hoop dreams

Modern Hand Embroidery

Cristin Morgan

Abrams, New York

For Abrams
Editor: Emma Jacobs
Cover Design: Deb Wood
Design Manager: Danny Maloney
Production Managers: Lindsay Bleemer and Kathy Lovisolo

Library of Congress Control Number: 2017944958

ISBN: 978-1-4197-2926-3
eISBN: 978-1-68335-219-8

Printed and bound in China
10 9 8 7 6 5 4 3 2 1

Abrams books are available at special discounts when purchased in quantity for premiums and promotions as well as fundraising or educational use. Special editions can also be created to specification. For details, contact specialsales@abramsbooks.com or the address below.

ABRAMS The Art of Books
195 Broadway, New York, NY 10007
abramsbooks.com

Conceived, designed, and produced by Quarto Publishing, an imprint of The Quarto Group
6 Blundell Street
London N7 9BH

For Quarto
Editor: Kate Burkett
Senior Art Editor: Emma Clayton
Designer: Karin Skanberg
Photography: Nicki Dowey and Phil Wilkins
Art Director: Caroline Guest
Creative Director: Moira Clinch
Publisher: Sam Warrington

QUAR.MDEM

FSC

MIX
Paper from responsible sources
FSC® C104723

CONTENTS

Meet Cristin

I can still remember my very first embroidery project: a celestially inspired half sun, half moon piece for a middle school art class. I worked on it during bus rides to and from school for a week or two, head down, lost in my own world, clutching my large hoop in one hand and a plastic needle and acrylic yarn in the other. I remember marveling at the way the stitches combined to make something tangible and textural appear out of what was once just a hand-sketched design on a piece of white fabric. It was like magic. I think that piece won an award in my school's art show that year, but even more memorable were those bus rides spent practicing new techniques. It was during those precious few moments each day that I fell in love with embroidery.

Since then, my love for embroidery has only grown. Through lots of practice and curious experimentation, I honed my skills. I've dabbled in other crafts throughout the years, including sewing, knitting, and felt work, but I always find myself drawn back to needlework. Even on days that feel endless, I look forward to quiet evenings curled up on the couch with my needle and thread. Embroidery is my creative outlet, my therapy, and a source of great joy.

The thing I love most about contemporary embroidery is the freedom. You don't need to master countless ancient techniques in order to create something beautiful. With just a few simple stitches, some basic materials, and a few extra minutes each day, you can stitch just about anything. I love using playful patterns and bold color palettes to bring even the simplest of motifs to life. Modern embroidery can be both beautiful and functional, and I strive to create pieces that can be enjoyed in everyday life.

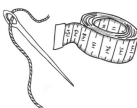

Whether you're BRAND NEW to the world of embroidery or an EXPERIENCED STITCHER, I hope this book will inspire you to pick up a needle!

i hope this book will inspire you

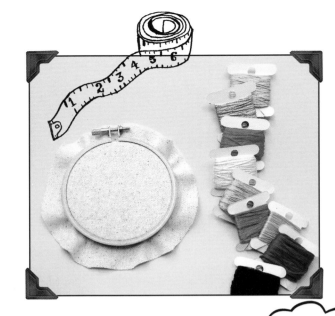

These are a few of my favorite things...

i love the freedom of contemporary EMBROIDERY

HAPPY PETS MAKE HAPPY HOOPS

A BLANK HOOP MEANS IT'S TIME FOR MAGIC!

In my happy place...

THE BELL JAR

I AM,
I AM,
I AM.

a source of great joy

TOOLS AND MATERIALS

If you're an experienced stitcher, you likely have many of these in your possession already. If you've never stitched before, don't worry—you don't need all of these things to get started. You can make a perfect starter kit with a hoop, a scrap of fabric, embroidery needles, scissors, and a few skeins of cotton floss!

THREAD

There are many different types of threads available for embroidery, and they come in a variety of materials and thicknesses. Each has its own characteristics and will produce different effects.

COTTON EMBROIDERY FLOSS

The most common type of embroidery thread. It comes in a wide range of colors and can be used for most types of embroidery. Embroidery floss consists of six twisted strands that can be divided or combined to achieve a desired thickness.

PEARL COTTON

Pearl cotton is also made of twisted strands, but unlike embroidery floss, it is non-divisible. It comes in many sizes, with size 3 being the thickest and size 12 being the finest. Pearl cotton has a glossy finish and can be found on spools or skeins in a wide range of colors.

METALLIC THREAD

Metallic thread is used to enhance embroidery with a glittery effect. These threads can be delicate and difficult to handle, so it's best to work with shorter lengths.

OTHER THREADS

Yarn, crewel thread, crochet and tapestry thread, ribbon, and sewing thread are also great options for adding texture and dimension to your embroidery. There are so many beautiful options out there. Don't be afraid to experiment!

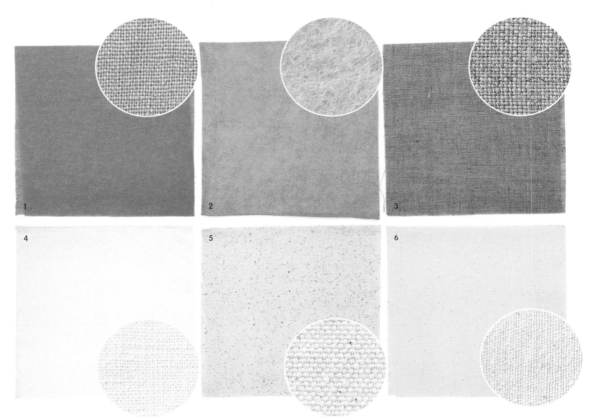

FABRICS

As with thread, there are endless options when it comes to choosing which type of fabric to embroider on. Almost any fabric can be suitable for embroidery, but some are easier to work with than others.

WOVENS

Woven fabrics cover a wide range and include any fabric made with horizontal and vertical threads. They are an excellent choice for embroidery since they keep their shape and are firm enough to support heavy stitches. Wovens come in an array of weights and types, ranging from lightweight—muslin (6) and quilters cotton (4 and 5)—to medium—linen (1 and 3)—and heavy weight—canvas and duck cloth.

FELT

Felt (2) is one of my favorite materials to work with because of its thickness and texture. It is available in a wide range of colors and thicknesses, and unlike woven fabrics, will not fray along the cut edges. It can be made from natural fibers such as wool, synthetic fibers like rayon or acrylic, or a blend of both. I generally prefer 100% wool or wool blended felt.

OTHER FABRICS

Other materials, such as knits and sheers, are a bit more difficult to work with but shouldn't be ruled out. To prepare stretchy or slippery fabric for embroidery, try adding a stabilizer (see *Stabilizers*, page 109). You can even embroider on more solid materials like paper or leather, but be sure to plan your stitches carefully, as any holes you make will be permanent.

READY-MADE ARTICLES

Embroidering on ready-made objects, such as backpacks, clothing, and linens, is an excellent way to personalize them and make them truly special. When choosing a piece to embroider, be sure to pay attention to the type of fabric it's made from.

NEEDLES

Needles come in a variety of lengths and thicknesses with different eyes and points, so select the type that suits the type of thread and fabric to be used. It's a good idea to

keep a selection of needles on hand so that you can switch as needed. If you notice that you're having trouble pulling your thread through your fabric, opt for a larger needle. Or, if you notice your needle leaving large holes in your fabric, opt for one that's a bit finer.

EMBROIDERY NEEDLES

Embroidery needles (2) have a medium length with a long eye and a sharp point. These are useful for most general embroidery. These are sized in reverse number order, so the higher the number, the finer the needle.

CHENILLE NEEDLES

Chenille needles (1) are longer and thicker than embroidery needles, with a large eye and a sharp point. These are useful for thicker threads, yarn, and ribbon.

TAPESTRY NEEDLES

Tapestry needles (3) are similar to chenille needles, but with a blunt point. These are useful for fabrics that have a looser weave.

SCISSORS

Although you can make do with just one good pair of scissors, having some options on hand will make your embroidery work a bit easier.

EMBROIDERY SCISSORS

Embroidery scissors are small and have a sharp point, making them ideal for snipping threads, removing unwanted stitches, and for small trimming tasks. I like to keep mine on a cord around my neck so that they're easy to keep track of as I work.

FABRIC SHEARS

A nice pair of fabric shears will make easy work of cutting out fabric. Be sure to use them only for cutting fabric though, as cutting other materials with them will cause them to dull quickly.

ALL PURPOSE SCISSORS

I like to keep a pair of regular household scissors handy for cutting out patterns, carbon paper, interfacing, etc.

EMBROIDERY HOOPS

An embroidery hoop holds your fabric taut as you stitch, which allows for even stitching and prevents puckering. I almost always use a hoop when stitching, except for when I stitch on felt and on ready-made garments with seams that might get in the way.

Hoops come in a variety of sizes, given by their diameter. Whenever possible, choose one that can hold the entire design so the hoop does not need to be shifted. For larger pieces greater than 10 in. (25 cm), quilting hoops are a bit wider and offer additional sturdiness.

MARKING TOOLS

LEAD PENCILS

Regular lead pencils are great to use for marking fabric. The marks they leave are light and, if not covered by your stitches, can be erased.

CHALK PENCILS

Chalk pencils are a good choice for marking on dark fabrics. Any uncovered marks can be easily brushed away once you've finished stitching.

WATER SOLUBLE PENS

Water soluble pens contain ink that disappears with water. Any marks that aren't fully covered with stitches can be removed with a damp cloth or cold water rinse.

AIR SOLUBLE PENS

Also called "disappearing ink" pens, these contain ink that fades gradually.

OTHER HELPFUL TOOLS

HOT GLUE GUN AND GLUE STICKS

Useful for finishing the backs of embroidery hoops and for other general use.

FABRIC GLUE

Glue for adhering layers of fabric. Choose a type that is washable for a permanent bond.

FRAY PREVENTER

A clear, liquid sealant that prevents cut edges of fabric from fraying.

MEASURING TAPE OR RULER

SEWING PINS OR CLIPS

IRON

THIMBLES

Used to protect your fingers.

TRACING PAPER AND CARDSTOCK

Useful for transferring designs and making templates.

CORNER PUSHING TOOL

A pointed object useful for turning corners in sewing projects. A large knitting needle works nicely.

PLIERS

For assembling jewelry and other findings.

SEWING MACHINE AND THREAD

MASKING TAPE

Helps to keep fabric edges from fraying while you work.

PAINT AND BRUSHES

For adding detail to fabric or hoops.

IRON-ON PATTERN SHEETS

Included in the envelope in the back of this book.

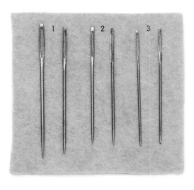

Chapter 1
JUST HOOPS

"HELLO" HOOP

One of my favorite things about embroidery is the texture the stitches create when they're piled together on the fabric, filling a once empty space. Here, a vivid color palette and highly textured fill stitch add visual interest to a simple handwritten message. Experiment with thread and fabric colors that appeal to you, or try using a patterned fabric to add a fun, graphic element to your work.

MATERIALS

- Transfer and marking tools
- 10 x 10-in. (25 x 25-cm) square of linen or cotton fabric
- 10 x 10-in. (25 x 25-cm) square of unbleached muslin (optional; see *Techniques*, page 109)
- 6-in. (15-cm) embroidery hoop
- Cotton embroidery floss
- Embroidery needle
- Scissors
- Backing materials

THREAD COLORS USED

- Golden olive, 6 strands
- Plum, 6 strands

FINISHED SIZE

- Diameter: 6 in. (15 cm)

Long and short stitch
(see page 113)

Back stitch
(see page 114)

1 Transfer the "hello" motif (see *Templates*, page 116) on to the piece of linen or cotton fabric (see *Techniques*, pages 107–108). Assemble the hoop (see *Techniques*, page 109), placing the piece of muslin (if using) underneath the main piece of fabric.

2 Fill the heavy strokes in each letter with a combination of long and short stitches.

3 Finish and connect each letter using back stitch. Adjust the stitch length as required, using shorter stitches around tight curves and longer stitches for straighter lines.

Finish the back of the hoop as desired (see *Finishing Your Hoop*, pages 46–47, for materials and methods).

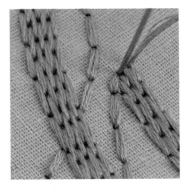

TIP *I've used six strands, but you can decrease the number of strands if you wish. Fewer strands will result in a more seamless, less chunky look, which would work well if you're using a patterned fabric.*

CONFETTI HOOP

This project is great for using up leftover pieces of thread, since you won't need much of each color (and the more colors you incorporate, the better!). I've provided two different methods for achieving the effect of freshly thrown confetti fluttering to the ground. Try one or both because, unlike the real thing, this confetti needs no cleanup! You can leave the wood natural or paint the hoop for an extra pop of color.

MATERIALS

- Marking tool
- 8 x 8-in. (20 x 20-cm) square of white quilter's cotton
- 8 x 8-in. (20 x 20-cm) square of unbleached muslin (optional; see *Techniques*, page 109)
- 4-in. (10-cm) embroidery hoop
- Cotton and metallic embroidery floss
- Embroidery needle
- Scissors
- Acrylic paint
- Foam brush
- Backing materials

THREAD COLORS USED

- Apricot, 4 strands
- Aquamarine, 4 strands
- Carnation, 4 strands
- Ecru, 4 strands
- Jade, 4 strands
- Lemon, 4 strands
- Plum, 4 strands
- Precious metal gold, 4 strands
- Royal blue, 4 strands
- Salmon, 4 strands
- Sky blue, 4 strands
- Violet, 4 strands

FINISHED SIZE

- Diameter: 4 in. (10 cm)

French knot (see page 112)

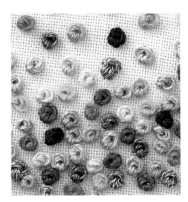  

1 Assemble the hoop (see *Techniques*, page 109), placing the piece of muslin (if using) underneath the square of cotton. Lightly mark a pattern of French knots on the main piece of fabric, concentrating the marks more heavily at the bottom of the hoop. (You can also opt to stitch this design freehand rather than marking your fabric.) Choose one thread color to begin with. Sew French knots, placing the colors randomly throughout the design. Remove the stitched fabric from the hoop.

2 To create the second confetti hoop, follow the instructions on the stitch and color placement in Step 1, but use straight stitches (see *Stitch Directory*, page 111), rather than French knots.

3 Paint the outer hoop, making sure to leave the inner edge (i.e. the part that will touch the fabric) clear of paint. Apply two or three coats. Allow the hoop to dry fully before reassembling.

Reassemble the hoop and finish the back as desired (see *Finishing Your Hoop*, pages 46–47, for materials and methods).

TIP *When stitching, aim to finish one color completely before moving on to the next. You can always come back and add more of any color you wish until your confetti is to your liking.*

WILDFLOWERS HOOP

Reminiscent of a traditional stitch sampler, this lovely hoop combines several basic stitches to create various decorative effects. The result is a beautiful burst of colorful flowers and foliage that has loads of texture and is sure to serve as a year-round reminder of warm and sunny spring days. Feel free to experiment with different stitch techniques from those listed here, to achieve your own unique version.

MATERIALS

- Transfer and marking tools
- 9 x 9-in. (23 x 23-cm) square of linen fabric
- 5-in. (13-cm) embroidery hoop
- Cotton embroidery floss
- Embroidery needle
- Scissors
- Backing materials

THREAD COLORS USED

- Coral, 4 strands
- Ecru, 4 strands
- Golden olive, 4 strands
- Hunter green, 4 strands
- Peach, 4 strands
- Moss green, 4 strands
- Straw, 6 strands
- Topaz, 4 strands

FINISHED SIZE

- Diameter: 5 in. (13 cm)

Back stitch
(see page 114)

Detached chain
stitch (see Chain
stitch, page 115)

French knot
(see page 112)

French knot
(wrapped three times;
see page 112)

Fern stitch
(see page 114)

Lazy daisy stitch
(see Chain stitch,
page 115)

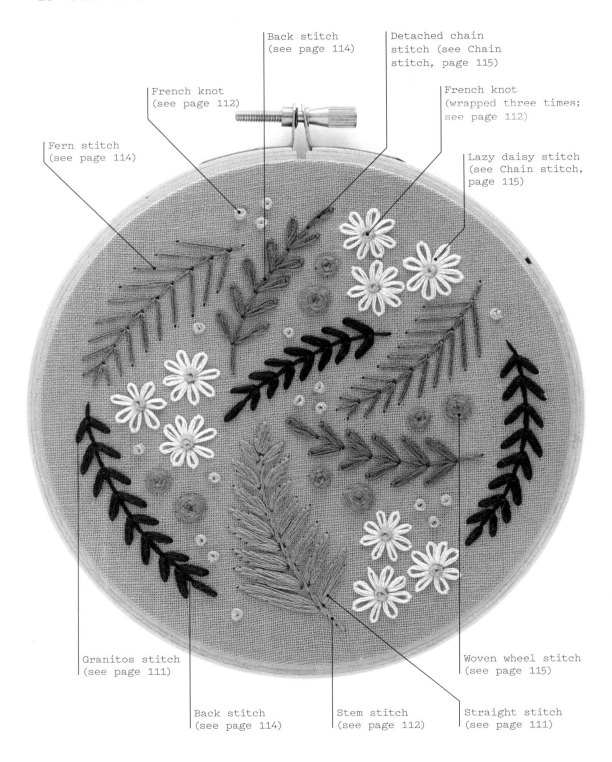

Granitos stitch
(see page 111)

Woven wheel stitch
(see page 115)

Back stitch
(see page 114)

Stem stitch
(see page 112)

Straight stitch
(see page 111)

1 Transfer the flower/foliage motifs (see *Templates*, page 116) on to the piece of linen fabric (see *Techniques*, pages 107–108). Assemble the hoop (see *Techniques*, page 109).

2 Stitch the flower and foliage motifs as shown, following any stitch order you like. Finish the back of the hoop as desired (see *Finishing Your Hoop*, pages 46–47, for materials and methods).

RAINBOW HOOP

This motif was inspired by a painting of a rainbow by my son. His paint dripped delightfully from the ends of the rainbow, as if the bright colors just couldn't be contained. That painting has earned a permanent spot on our wall—a beautiful and innocent reminder that there is always light somewhere. This project echoes that sentiment. I used chain stitch to create bold lines of bright color and a fringe to extend the rainbow outside the hoop. Oval hoops are super fun to work with, too, and offer an unexpected background shape for your embroidery.

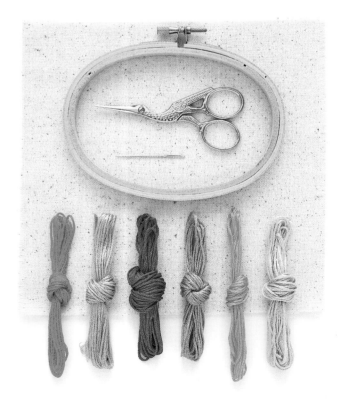

MATERIALS

- Transfer and marking tools
- 7 x 9-in. (18 x 23-cm) piece of linen or cotton fabric
- 7 x 9-in. (18 x 23-cm) piece of muslin (optional; see *Techniques*, page 109)
- 3 x 5-in. (7.5 x 13-cm) embroidery hoop
- Cotton embroidery floss
- Embroidery needle
- Scissors
- Ruler
- Backing materials

THREAD COLORS USED (FOR HOOP SHOWN)

- Apricot, 6 strands
- Blue-green, 6 strands
- Carnation, 6 strands
- Desert sand, 6 strands
- Plum, 6 strands
- Shell pink, 6 strands

FINISHED SIZE

- 3 x 5 in. (7.5 x 13 cm)

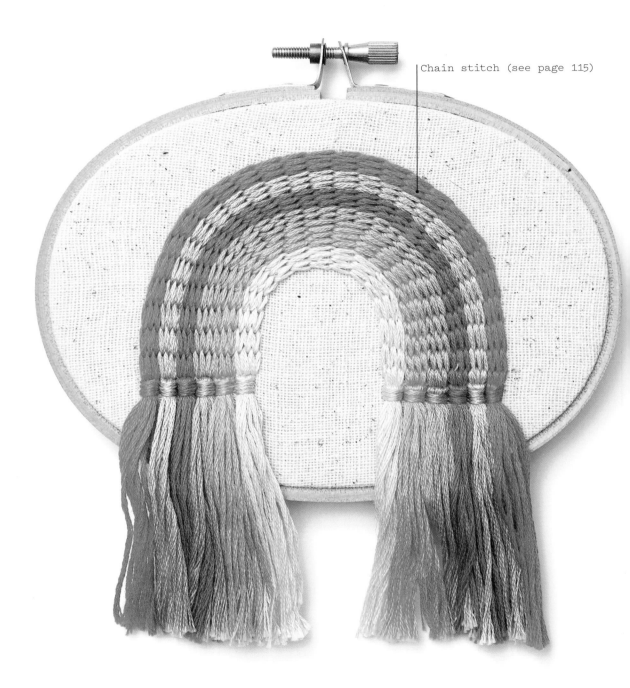

Chain stitch (see page 115)

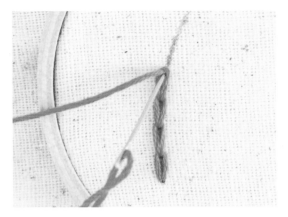

1 Transfer the rainbow motif (see *Templates*, page 117) onto the piece of linen or cotton fabric (see *Techniques*, pages 107–108). Only mark the top line, as this will be your guide for all of the rows. Assemble the hoop (see *Techniques*, page 109) and begin stitching. Sew one row of chain stitch along the marked line. Make the stitch length about ¼ in. (6 mm).

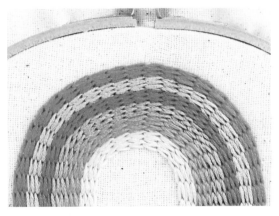

2 Stitch two additional rows of chain stitch close to the first row with the same color, to make a total of three rows in the first color. Repeat for the five remaining stripes of the rainbow.

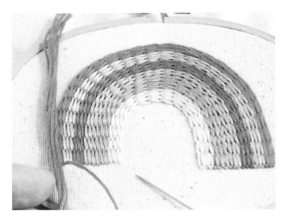

3 Prepare the fringe using the same floss colors you used to stitch the stripes. Measure and cut ten 7-in. (18-cm) pieces of thread per color. Separate into two groups of five pieces of thread per color. You will use one group of five pieces for each end of the rainbow.

4 To attach the fringe, start with the outermost stripe. Place five pieces of thread over the first stripe, with the center of the threads positioned at the bottom of the stripe.

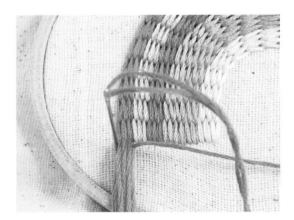

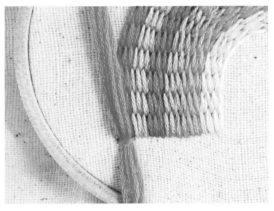

5 Use matching floss to secure the fringe. Bring your needle up and over the threads, as shown, then back down through the fabric, making one stitch to secure the fringe in position at the base of the stripe.

6 Pull this stitch taut.

7 Fold the threads down over the stitch and hold them in place with your non-stitching hand.

8 Bring your needle back up and over the threads, then back down through the fabric. Repeat a few more times to fully fasten the fringe.

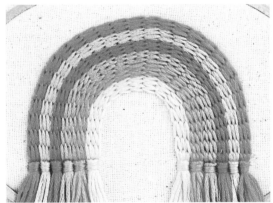

9 Secure the fringe threads with a knot at the back of the embroidery hoop.

10 Repeat Steps 4–8 for each color, working from left to right so that the needle always comes up on the open side and down on the side with the previously attached fringe. Trim the fringe to the desired length. Finish the back of the hoop as desired (see *Finishing Your Hoop*, pages 46–47, for materials and methods), taking care not to snip the fringe by mistake!

MONOGRAM HOOP

A bright floral burst can transform a simply stitched initial into a beloved keepsake. Adding a ribbon for hanging makes this small hoop suitable for use as a holiday ornament, but chances are it will be displayed all year round! Experiment with the floral embellishments to see how much the look changes when you just use greenery or a different type of flower. A set of these makes a lovely holiday gift.

MATERIALS

- Transfer and marking tools
- 8 x 8-in. (20 x 20-cm) square of cotton or linen fabric
- 8 x 8-in. (20 x 20-cm) square of unbleached muslin (optional; see *Techniques*, page 109)
- 4-in. (10-cm) embroidery hoop
- Cotton embroidery floss
- Embroidery needle
- Scissors
- Backing materials
- 15-in. (38-cm) piece of ribbon, string, or trim (optional)

THREAD COLORS USED

- Blue-green, 6 strands
- Ecru, 6 strands
- Golden olive, 6 strands
- Melon, 6 strands
- Peach, 6 strands

FINISHED SIZE

- Diameter: 4 in. (10 cm)

Back stitch
(see page 114)

Straight stitch
(see page 111)

French knot
(see page 112)

Woven wheel stitch
(see page 115)

1 Transfer the floral motif (see *Templates*, page 117) on to the cotton or linen fabric (see *Techniques*, pages 107–108). Assemble the hoop (see *Techniques*, page 109), placing the piece of muslin (if using) underneath the main fabric, and start stitching. For the flowers, stitch three woven wheels and add a few French knots to the centers. Add a tiny cluster of French knots between the flowers.

2 For the leaves, make a long straight stitch from the base of the top leaf to the side of the flower, where the leaves meet. Stitch two leaves using straight stitch, following the outline of the leaf as the starting point and ending all the stitches at the same point. The two leaves at the base will overlap slightly. Stitch the top leaf in the same way.

3 For the letter, stitch using back stitch. Finish the back of the hoop as desired (see *Finishing Your Hoop*, pages 46–47, for materials and methods). Attach the piece of ribbon, string, or trim (if using).

TIP *I made my back stitches extra-long and added a second line to the outer strokes of the letter, but you could also stitch the letter using shorter strokes or a different stitch altogether.*

BUZZING BEES HOOP

The fuzzy bees in this design look as if they're about to buzz right out of the hoop, thanks to the three-dimensional quality of the padded satin stitch and French knot fill. These bees are perfect in a hoop, but they would also look great stitched onto a denim jacket or sweatshirt.

MATERIALS

- Transfer and marking tools
- 10 x 10-in. (25 x 25-cm) square of linen or cotton fabric
- 10 x 10-in. (25 x 25-cm) square of unbleached muslin (optional; see *Techniques*, page 109)
- 6-in. (15-cm) embroidery hoop
- Cotton embroidery floss
- Pearl cotton, size 12
- Embroidery needle
- Scissors
- Backing materials

THREAD COLORS USED

- Black, 4 strands for stripes and head; 6 strands for French knots
- Straw, 4 strands
- Pearl cotton, black

FINISHED SIZE

- Diameter: 6 in. (15 cm)

Satin stitch with
split stitch padding
(see Satin stitch and
note, page 113)

French knot
(see page 112)

Straight stitch
(see page 111)

Granitos stitch
(see page 111)

Back stitch
(see page 114)

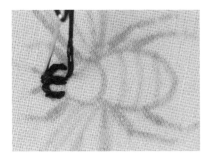

1 Transfer the bee motifs (see *Templates*, page 117) on to the square of linen or cotton fabric (see *Techniques*, pages 107–108). Assemble the hoop (see *Techniques*, page 109), placing the muslin (if using) underneath the main fabric. Sew a border of split stitch along the top of each bee's head. Satin stitch over this line, beginning where the head meets the body and working outward to cover the sewn border of satin stitch. Work from the center over to one side, then finish the other side. Stitch the stripes in the same way.

2 Fill the middle body segment with French knots. Start at the center and work outward and around.

3 Use the pearl cotton for the bees' legs. Make a granitos stitch with three passes for the segments closest to the body, followed by a granitos stitch with two passes for the middle segment. Finish with a single straight stitch for the outermost segment. For the front legs and antennae, make a granitos stitch with two passes for the segments closest to the body, then a single straight stitch for the outermost segment.

4 Using pearl cotton, outline the wings of the bees with back stitch. Finish the back of the hoop as desired (see *Finishing Your Hoop*, pages 46–47, for materials and methods).

TIP *Padding your satin stitch with a split-stitch border underneath gives it a more defined and slightly raised edge, but regular satin stitch would work just fine if you want to skip the extra step.*

PEACE AND NAIL POLISH HOOP

Here, the iconic symbol of peace and friendship gets a fun update in the form of a colorful thread manicure. This is a great project for beginners, since it only uses a few simple stitches and offers plenty of room for embellishment. You can stitch the design as shown here, or use different filling and outlining techniques to achieve various effects.

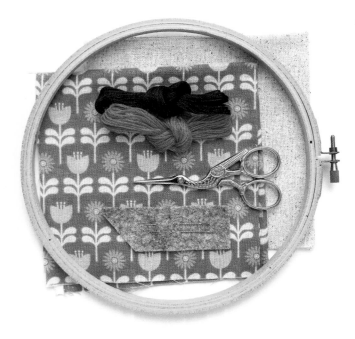

MATERIALS

- Transfer and marking tools
- 10 x 10-in (25 x 25-cm) square of solid cotton fabric
- 10 x 10-in (25 x 25-cm) square of muslin (optional; see *Techniques*, page 109)
- 7-in. (18-cm) embroidery hoop
- Cotton embroidery floss
- Embroidery needle
- Scissors
- Backing materials

THREAD COLORS USED

- Black, 3 strands
- Bright red, 4 strands

FINISHED SIZE

- Diameter: 7 in. (18 cm)

Satin stitch
(see page 113)

Back stitch
(see page 114)

1 Transfer the hand motif
(see *Templates*, page 118)
on to the piece of cotton
fabric (see *Techniques*,
pages 107-108). Assemble the
hoop (see *Techniques*, page
109), placing the square of
muslin (if using) underneath
the main piece of fabric.

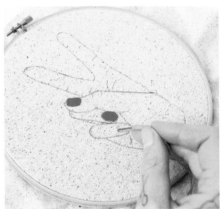

2 Fill in the red nails
with satin stitch. For
each nail, begin the satin
stitch in the middle and
work your way completely to
one side, then the other.

3 Fill in the outlines
of the hand in black
with back stitch. Adjust
the stitch length as
needed, using shorter
stitches around tight
curves, such as nails
and fingertips, and longer
stitches for straighter
lines. Finish the back
of the hoop as desired
(see *Finishing Your Hoop*,
pages 46-47, for materials
and methods).

FINISHING YOUR HOOP

Embroidery hoops aren't just useful for keeping fabric in place while you stitch. They also make excellent frames for your finished work! It only takes a few simple steps to turn your work in progress into a ready-to-hang work of art.

My stitches usually end up quite messy on the backside, so I like to use a piece of fabric to cover them. I choose something with a fun print for an unexpected touch, but you can use just about anything. Solid fabric or felt are great choices if you wish to add a personalized message, such as a name or date, to the back of the hoop. This is a great way to use up pieces of fabric from your stash that are too small for larger projects. If you prefer, you can omit the backing fabric and just finish the edges of your work, leaving the stitches exposed.

1 Remove the embroidered fabric from the hoop. If you have used a piece of lining fabric, you'll have two pieces of fabric stitched together. Cut a piece of fabric that's approximately the same size as the embroidered piece. If it's a little smaller, that's okay! Just make sure there's enough fabric to fit in the hoop and wrap around the edge. Place the piece of backing fabric face down on a flat surface, then center the embroidered piece on top, facing up.

2 Loosen the screw on the outer ring of the embroidery hoop. Reassemble the hoop with all the layers of fabric. Tighten the screw halfway and adjust the layers of fabric by pulling them gently and evenly. If necessary, adjust the pieces of fabric individually. Make sure to keep the design centered and avoid distorting it. Once it is centered and the fabric is smooth and taut, tighten the screw all the way, to stop anything from shifting.

TIP *If you would like to add a personalized message, stitch it onto the piece of backing fabric. Make sure to place the message in a spot that won't be covered by the embroidery hoop.*

3 Turn the hoop over. Trim away the backing fabric and optional liner fabric, getting as close to the edge of the hoop as possible. Be careful not to cut through the embroidered fabric accidentally.

4 Trim around the piece of embroidered fabric, leaving just enough excess so that the fabric can wrap around the edge of the hoop. This is usually about ½–¾ in. (12–18 mm).

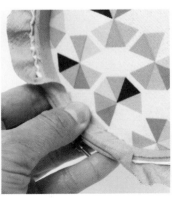

5 Working in short sections, about 2–3 in. (5–8 cm) at a time, use a hot glue gun to apply a line of glue to the inner edge of the hoop. Let cool for a few seconds, then use your fingers to press the fabric around the edge of the hoop and over the glue. Repeat, working around the hoop until the edge of the fabric has been completely secured.

Chapter 2

FOR YOUR HOME

LETTER FLAG BANNER

Soft felt provides a durable background for these endlessly customizable letter flags, which add a personal touch to any special event or holiday, or even to everyday decor. Split stitch is my absolute favorite for lettering because it results in smooth, uninterrupted lines, but you can also use other stitches, such as back or chain stitch, depending on your preference.

MATERIALS

- Tracing paper
- Transfer and marking tools
- Cardstock or posterboard
- Tape
- Scissors
- Ruler
- Three to four 9 x 12-in. (23 x 30-cm) sheets of felt (either wool, wool-blend, or eco)
- Cotton embroidery floss
- Embroidery needle (larger size works best on felt)
- Sewing pins
- Sewing machine
- Sewing thread (to match the felt)
- Cotton cord (I used about 2 yd / 1.8 m for a banner of 8 flags, including 3 in. (7.5 cm) of cord for each flag and 32 in. (80 cm) for the beads and knots (i.e., 16 in. / 40 cm at each end), plus the desired amount of excess in between the knots and flags to reach the desired length of banner)

- Crochet hook or wooden skewer (optional)
- Six 25-mm unfinished wood beads

STITCH USED

- Split stitch (see page 111)

THREAD COLORS USED

- Aquamarine, 6 strands
- Bright red, 6 strands
- Coral, 6 strands
- Peach, 6 strands
- Light gold, 6 strands
- Straw, 6 strands

FINISHED SIZE

- Each flag: 3 x 4 in. (7.5 x 10 cm)
- Total banner length: 50 in. (1.27 m)

1 Trace the flag template (see *Templates*, page 125) onto a piece of tracing paper and cut out. Place the cut-out on a piece of cardstock or posterboard and tape in place to secure, then draw around the edges. Flip the cut-out over, keeping the top aligned with the top of the flag you just traced, as shown. Tape in place once more, and trace again. Cut out the template.

2 Using the cardstock / posterboard template, lightly trace the flags onto the sheets of felt. You should be able to fit three or four flags onto each sheet. Trace and carefully cut out the desired number of flags (i.e., one flag for each letter of the banner), plus one for any blank spaces you need.

3 Fold each flag in half so that the top and bottom points meet. Press your fingers along the fold to mark the center of the flag, then unfold and mark this center line with a pin. Measure 1 in. (2.5 cm) down from the line and mark with another pin—this is where you will align the tops of the letters.

4 Transfer the letters to the flags (see *Templates*, pages 120-121). Center each letter, adding one to each flag, making sure to align the top of each letter with the lower pin mark.

5 Stitch each letter using split stitch. I like to nestle a second line of split stitch just beside the first to achieve a bolder line.

6 Fold the flags in half again and pin together. Sew each flag with a 1/2-in. (12-mm) margin at the top and a 1/4-in. (6-mm) margin around the edges, removing the pins as you sew.

TIP *Before sewing the flags in Step 6, practice on some scrap pieces of felt to check that the thread tension and stitch-length settings on your sewing machine are correct. If you don't have a sewing machine, hand stitch with running stitch (see page 114).*

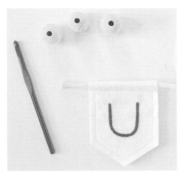

7 To assemble the banner, wrap a piece of tape tightly around both ends of the cotton cord. Thread the flags onto the cord in the correct order. This should be possible with just the taped end of cord, but if you find it difficult, tape the cord to a thin crochet hook or wooden skewer and thread the flags onto the cord in that way instead.

8 After all of the flags have been assembled on the cord, finish the ends. Starting at one end, tie a knot approximately 16 in. (40 cm) from the end of the cord. String three wooden beads onto the cord.

9 Secure the beads with an Overhand Knot, leaving a loop for hanging (see below).

MAKING AN OVERHAND KNOT WITH A LOOP

10 Repeat Steps 8-9 at the other end of the banner. Neatly trim the ends of the cords.

1 Fold the end of the cord to form a loop, holding the cord roughly where you want the final knot to be.

2 Fold the loop over and tuck the looped end over and through the center. Tighten the loop halfway, leaving the knot loose enough to make adjustments. Check the cords are parallel and the knot is in the right place. Pull the knot tight.

WINK PILLOW

Add a bit of intrigue to your favorite space with these winking eyes! The envelope closure makes changing the look of your pillow really easy. Using wool embroidery thread gives this design added durability and a soft, cozy touch, but regular cotton floss would work just as well, too.

MATERIALS

- Transfer and marking tools
- 13 x 17-in. (33 x 43-cm) piece of canvas fabric
- Two 13 x 11-in. (33 x 28-cm) pieces of printed cotton fabric
- 6-in. (15-cm) embroidery hoop
- Wool embroidery thread (100% merino wool) or lightweight yarn
- Embroidery needle (with a large eye)
- Iron
- Scissors
- Sewing machine
- Sewing thread (to match the fabric)
- Sewing pins
- 16 x 12-in. (40 x 30-cm) pillow form

STITCHES USED

- Back stitch (see page 114)
- Satin stitch (see page 113)

THREAD COLOR USED

- Black

FINISHED SIZE

- 16 x 12 in. (40 x 30 cm)

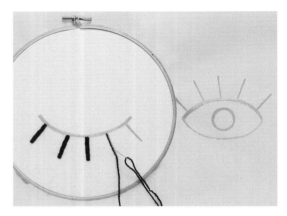

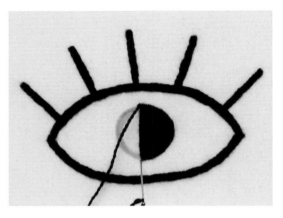

1 Mark a 13 x 17-in. (33 x 43-cm) rectangle on the piece of canvas fabric. Transfer the eye motifs (see *Templates*, page 119) to the center of the marked rectangle (see *Techniques*, pages 107–108). Assemble the fabric in the hoop (see *Techniques*, page 109), placing the closed eye in the hoop first. Stitch the eyelashes and eyelid of the closed eye with wool thread, using four to five rows of back stitch. Try to stagger your stitches a bit so that they don't begin and end at the same points.

2 Assemble the fabric for the open eye in the hoop. Stitch the eyelashes and upper and lower eyelids with back stitch, as in Step 1. Use satin stitch to fill the pupil of the eye.

3 Remove the stitched fabric from the hoop and use the iron to press out the wrinkles. Cut the canvas fabric to size along the marked line.

4 Cut two 13 x 11-in. (33 x 28-cm) pieces from the printed fabric and hem one long edge of each piece. To do this, fold in the edge by 1/2 in. (12 mm), press to crease, then fold in another 1/2 in. (12 mm) to enclose the raw edge. Machine stitch in place.

TIP *If you would like your pillow cover to be washable, pre-wash, dry, and iron the fabric first.*

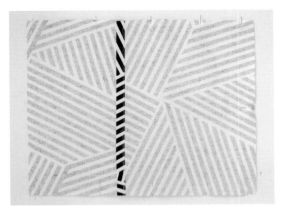

5 Place the embroidered piece of canvas on a flat surface with the right side facing up. Place one of the hemmed back pieces on top of the embroidered piece, right side facing down, ensuring that the raw edges are aligned and the hemmed side is facing the center.

6 Place the other hemmed back piece over the other two pieces of fabric, with the raw edges aligned on the opposite side and the hemmed side facing the center (as shown). There should be a few inches of overlap between the two back pieces. Pin the pieces of fabric together.

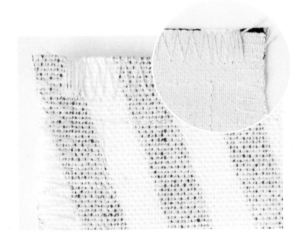

7 Machine stitch around the edges, using a 1/2-in. (12-mm) seam allowance. Remove the pins. Switch the sewing machine to a zigzag setting and stitch all around the edges again, so that the needle comes down just past the edge of the fabric. This will stop the edges from fraying.

8 Turn the pillow case right side out and push out the corners. Insert your pillow form and adjust as needed.

CACTUS CLOTH NAPKINS

Cloth napkins offer an attractive and eco-friendly alternative to paper ones. The second layer of fabric for the back of these napkins covers and protects the stitches and makes them reversible. Try mixing up your fabric selection or thread colors for a mismatched set, or coordinate your choices with your existing decor.

MATERIALS

- Transfer and marking tools
- For the top: 7 x 7-in. (18 x 18-cm) square of cotton or linen fabric (prewashed and pressed)
- For the bottom: 7 x 7-in. (18 x 18-cm) square of cotton or linen fabric (prewashed and pressed)
- 4-in. (10-cm) embroidery hoop
- Cotton embroidery floss
- Embroidery needle
- Iron
- Scissors
- Sewing pins
- Sewing machine
- Sewing thread (to match the fabric)
- Point turner or other pointed object, e.g., chopstick, knitting needle

STITCHES USED

- Back stitch (see page 114)
- Straight stitch (see page 111)

THREAD COLOR USED

- Black, 3 strands

FINISHED SIZE

- Each napkin: 6 x 6 in. (15 x 15 cm)

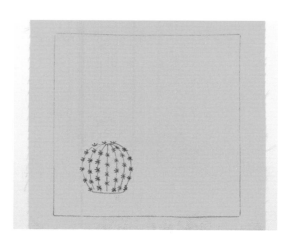

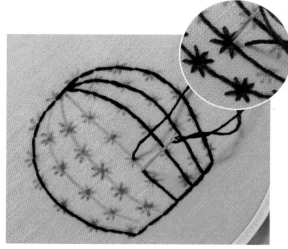

1 For each napkin, mark a 7-in. (18-cm) square on the top piece of fabric (see *Techniques*, pages 107–108). Transfer the cactus motif (see *Templates*, page 118) onto the fabric, positioning it in the lower left corner, 1 in. (2.5 cm) from the edge.

2 Assemble the fabric in the hoop (see *Techniques*, page 109). Use the black embroidery floss to stitch the main outlines of the cactus motif with back stitch. Create the rows of cactus prickles with straight stitch.

3 Remove the fabric from the hoop, use an iron to press out any wrinkles, and cut out the napkin along the marked lines.

4 Mark and cut out a 7-in. (18-cm) square of bottom fabric. Pin the pieces of embroidered fabric and bottom fabric together, with the right sides facing in.

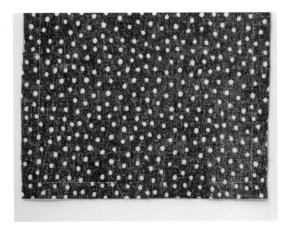

5 Use the sewing machine to stitch around the edges with a ½-in. (12-mm) seam allowance. Leave an opening about 2 in. (5 cm) wide for turning the napkin right side out.

6 Trim the corners of the napkin, taking care not to snip into your stitching.

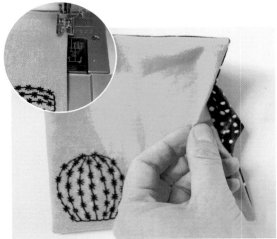

7 Turn the napkin right side out through the opening. Use a point turner or other pointed object to push out all the corners and seams neatly.

8 Tuck in the edges of the opening, press with the iron, and use the sewing machine to topstitch around all four sides, approximately ⅛ in. (3 mm) from the edge.

STRIPED PLANT COZY

I have a habit of bringing home more houseplants than I know what to do with. While I'm always happy to find space for new additions, I almost never have enough pots! These fabric planters provide the perfect solution. They're simple to make, and the pattern can easily be sized up or down. If you like, choose a brightly colored liner fabric and fold down the top to expose a punch of color to contrast with the neutral stitched stripes.

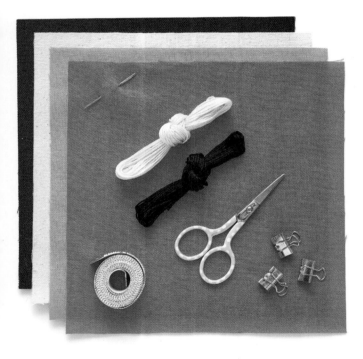

MATERIALS

- Transfer and marking tools
- 17 x 9-in. (43 x 23-cm) piece of duck cloth
- 17 x 9-in. (43 x 23-cm) piece of lightweight cotton liner fabric
- Cardstock or posterboard
- Tape
- Ruler
- Scissors
- Cotton embroidery floss
- Embroidery needle
- Sewing pins or binder clips
- Sewing machine
- Sewing thread (to match the cloth)
- Iron

STITCH USED

- Back stitch (see page 114)

THREAD COLOR USED

- Black, 6 strands
- Ecru, 6 strands

FINISHED SIZE

- 4 x 6 in. (10 x 15 cm)

1 Before making the cozy template, enlarge the design (see *Templates*, page 123) by approximately 400 percent so it measures 8¼ x 8¾ in. (21 x 22 cm). Place the template on a sheet of cardstock or posterboard and tape in place. Using a ruler, draw around the template once more. Cut out, marking the side that says "fold."

2 Fold the duck cloth in half so it measures 8½ x 9 in. (21.5 x 23 cm). Align the template along the fold and mark the outline, then flip the cloth and repeat on the other side. Cut out. Repeat for the liner fabric. Mark lines for the stripes on the duck cloth, spacing them about 1 in. (2.5 cm) apart and beginning roughly 1½ in. (4 cm) from the top.

3 Stitch the black stripes using back stitch, making each stitch approximately ¼-½ in. (6-12 mm) long. Stop about ⅛-¼ in. (3-6 mm) from each side.

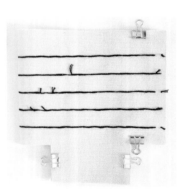

4 Fold the duck cloth in half, with the right side facing in, and pin or clip together.

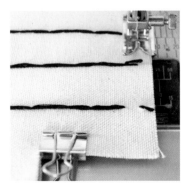

5 Sew on a sewing machine, using a ¼-in. (6-mm) seam allowance on the side and a ½-in. (12-mm) allowance along the bottom. Do not stitch around the cut-out corners. Press the bottom and side seams open.

6 Pinch the unsewn corners together and pull the cozy apart, adjoining the side and bottom seams.

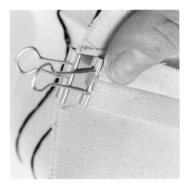

7 Pin or clip the seams together, then sew using a ¼-in. (6-mm) seam allowance.

8 Repeat on the other side of the cozy to make the bottom square. Repeat Steps 5–7 to make the liner.

9 Turn the exterior fabric right side out. Fold the top edge inward by ½ in. (12 mm) and press with a hot iron. Repeat for the liner, but this time keep the right side facing in and fold the top edge over.

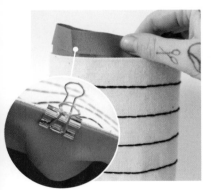

TIP *Always remove your plant for watering, and be sure to place something waterproof inside the cozy to prevent water staining and spoiling the fabric! A recycled plastic lid works nicely, as does a little plastic bag.*

10 Place the liner inside the exterior layer and pin or clip the top edges together, as shown.

11 Use a sewing machine to topstitch the exterior layer and liner together, close to the edge.

FRAMED FERN

This framed fern resembles one of those antique botanical prints, but with a dimensional and colorful twist. Framing embroidery is an easy way to give it a sophisticated upgrade. This simple method is achievable with just a few easy-to-find materials, and the result is so lovely. I prefer to frame my pieces without a glass cover, so that the texture of the stitches is visible. When framing a piece in this way, be sure to leave plenty of extra fabric around the design, as you'll need a bit more than is required when displaying embroidery in a hoop.

MATERIALS

- Transfer and marking tools
- 10 x 14-in. (25 x 35.5-cm) piece of speckled cotton fabric
- 7-in. (18-cm) embroidery hoop
- Cotton embroidery floss
- Embroidery needle
- Scissors
- Iron
- Metal ruler
- 5 x 7-in. (13 x 18-cm) picture frame
- Piece of foam board (slightly larger than the frame)
- Craft knife
- Stainless-steel pins

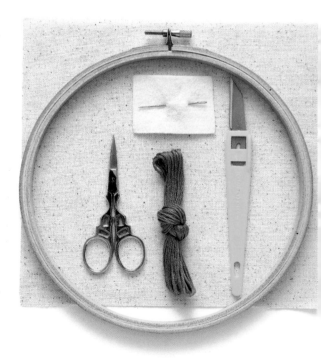

STITCHES USED

- Chain stitch / lazy daisy stitch (see page 115)
- Stem stitch (see page 112)
- Straight stitch (see page 111)

THREAD COLOR USED

- Aquamarine, 6 strands

FINISHED SIZE

- Depends on the frame size (this frame measures 5 x 7 in. / 13 x 18 cm)

1 Cut a piece of fabric approximately double the height and width of the frame opening. Using the glass from the frame as a guide, mark the opening in the center of the fabric. Enlarge the fern motif (see *Templates*, page 125) by approximately 133 percent so it measures 4¼ x 6¼ in. (11 x 16 cm) and transfer it to the fabric center (see *Techniques*, pages 107–108).

2 Assemble the fabric in the hoop (see *Techniques*, page 109), then begin embroidering the fern motif. For the fronds of the fern, stitch each leaf with a straight stitch first, then place a detached chain stitch (also known as a lazy daisy stitch) over each straight stitch. This results in a filled-in effect.

3 Use stem stitch to sew the main stem and also the frond stems. Remove the fabric from the hoop.

4 Iron the embroidery face down on a soft, smooth surface, gently pulling the fabric to smooth stubborn wrinkles or puckers.

5 Place the glass from the frame very carefully over the piece of foam board and trace around the edges.

6 Use the craft knife and metal ruler to trim the piece of foam board to size along the marked line.

TIP *Avoid ironing heavily over your stitches, as this can warp them. Instead, focus on smoothing the fabric only. If you still have a few wrinkles or puckers between the stitches, don't worry—the rest of the framing process should take care of this. (See Techniques, page 110 for more tips on ironing.)*

7 Place the piece of foam board in the frame to be sure it fits. There should be a little bit of wiggle room between the foam board and the inner edge of the frame, as you'll need some space for wrapping the fabric. If necessary, trim the foam board until it is the right size.

8 Place the embroidered fabric face down and center the foam board directly under the stitched motif. Turn over to check the design is centered and adjust as needed. Once the design is centered, insert one pin in each side, directly into the foam.

9 Beginning on one side, place pins approximately every ½ in. (12 mm). Work from the center out, pulling the fabric gently toward the back and sides as you go, to keep it smooth and taut. Repeat on the opposite side, then on the remaining two sides.

TIP *Don't push the pins all the way into the foam until you've pinned all the sides—leaving them inserted halfway makes it easier to remove them if you need to adjust the fabric to keep the fern centered.*

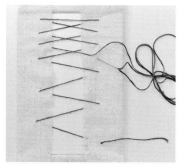

10 Once you've pinned all four sides and are satisfied that the fern is centered, push the pins in completely and add more so that the pins are spaced every ¼ in. (6 mm) or so. Working with two parallel sides at a time, fold the excess fabric over the foam board toward the back.

11 If necessary, trim the fabric so there are gaps between parallel edges. Cut a long piece of floss and thread it on a needle. Stitch the edges together, going back and forth between them as if you are lacing a shoe. Once you reach the top, go back down in the opposite direction.

12 Lightly pull the loose ends and tie them together. Repeat for the other two sides, folding in the corners as shown. Reassemble the frame without the glass.

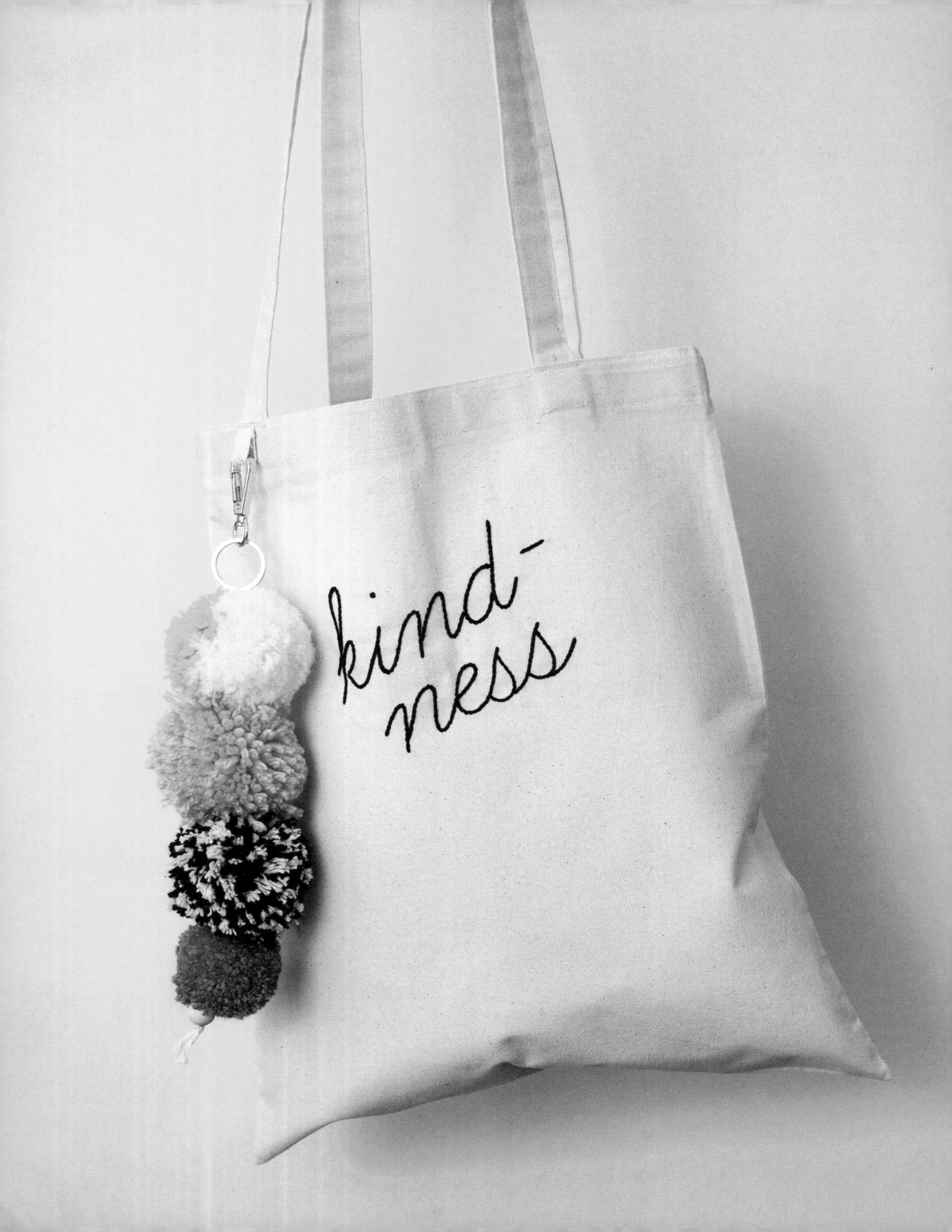
kind-
ness

Chapter 3

FOR YOU

FLORAL JACKET

This project is a perfect introduction to embroidering on clothing. Whether you stitch a single flower or a whole garden, these colorful blooms will give your garments a new lease on life. The flowers and leaves can be arranged to fit together depending on the space you have to work with, making this design suitable for any type and style of garment. I like to use all six strands of floss to make the design stand out from the fabric, but you could use fewer for a more delicate effect. Just remember that fewer strands means more stitches to achieve full coverage.

MATERIALS

- Transfer and marking tools
- Jacket or other garment
- Embroidery stabilizer (optional)
- Embroidery hoop (optional, as not necessary for heavyweight materials such as canvas or denim)
- Cotton embroidery floss
- Embroidery needle
- Scissors
- Sewing pins

STITCHES USED

- French knot (see page 112)
- Long and short stitch (see page 113)
- Split stitch (see page 111)

THREAD COLORS USED

- Apricot, 6 strands
- Blue-green, 6 strands
- Bright red, 6 strands
- Coral, 6 strands
- Golden olive, 6 strands
- Mauve, 6 strands
- Olive green, 6 strands
- Plum, 6 strands
- Shell pink, 6 strands
- Straw, 6 strands

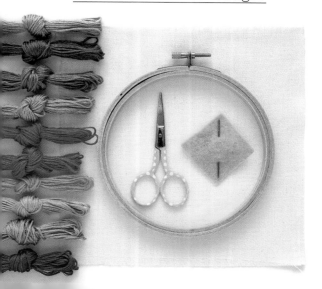

1 Transfer your choice of flower and foliage motifs (see *Templates*, page 125) to your garment, as desired (see *Techniques*, pages 107–108). I recommend starting small here—just mark a flower or two at first, as you can always add more as you go! This motif works well as a stencil, as it lets you place the flowers and leaves wherever they work best on your specific garment. I've used that method here.

2 Stabilize your garment if necessary. For tips on when and how to choose the right stabilizer for a garment, see *Techniques*, page 109. My jacket is medium-weight with a bit of stretch, so I used a medium-heavy weight cut-away stabilizer. Cut the stabilizer to the approximate size of the area you'll be stitching. Attach the stabilizer to the wrong side of the fabric, following the manufacturer's instructions.

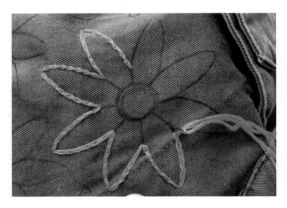

3 To stitch the flowers, begin by outlining the upper portion of each petal with split stitch.

4 Using the line of split stitch as your starting point, add a row of long and short stitches around each petal. Angle your stitches slightly toward the base of the petal as you work your way around.

TIP *Be sure your garment is clean and dry before you begin stitching, and press if necessary.*

5 If you wish, switch the thread color as you move toward the center and continue filling each petal with long and short stitches, keeping the stitches approximately the same length as the long stitches from the first row.

6 To stitch the centers of the flowers, fill the center of each with tightly spaced French knots. Begin in the center and work your way out and around.

7 To stitch the leaves, outline each leaf with a line of split stitch. Add a row of long and short stitches, using the split-stitch outline as a starting point. As you reach the base of the leaf, angle the stitches toward the middle, as shown, so that the stitches on each side of the leaf base meet at the center. Switch the thread color as you move toward the center, if you wish, and continue filling as in Step 5.

8 Remove the excess stabilizer as explained in the manufacturer's instructions. (To remove my cut-away stabilizer, I carefully trimmed around the edge of the motif with a small pair of scissors, making sure not to snip into any of my stitches.)

HEART COLLAR

A detachable collar is a super-fun way to update any outfit.
I love to wear these collars with a sweater for a layered
look without the bulk, or over a T-shirt for an unexpected
touch. Brightly colored hearts lend a punch of graphic charm
and texture to any ensemble, but a floral motif would also be
lovely. If you'd rather not sew your own collar, remove one
from an existing shirt and stitch directly on that instead.

MATERIALS

- Transfer and marking tools
- Collar top: piece of linen fabric
- Collar bottom: piece of cotton or
  linen fabric
- Lightweight fusible interfacing
- 6-in. (15-cm) embroidery hoop
- Cotton embroidery floss
- Pearl cotton, size 12
- Embroidery needle
- Scissors
- Iron
- Sewing machine
- Sewing thread (to match the fabric)
- Sewing pins
- Point turner or other pointed object,
  e.g., chopstick, knitting needle
- Two 24-in. (60-cm) pieces of trim or
  ribbon (for the tie)

STITCHES USED

- Back stitch (see page 114)
- Split stitch (see page 111)

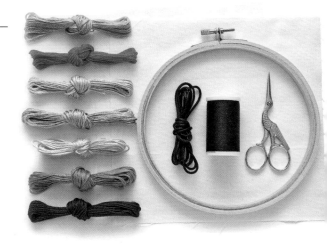

THREAD COLORS USED

- Cornflower blue, 6 strands
- Dark sea green, 6 strands
- Light sea green, 6 strands
- Mauve, 6 strands
- Peach, 6 strands
- Red, 6 strands
- Straw, 6 strands
- Pearl cotton, black

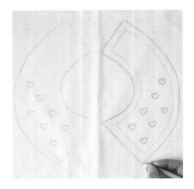

1 Mark two sides of the collar with the transferred heart motifs (see *Templates*, page 124) on the top fabric piece (see *Techniques*, pages 107-108). Reverse the pattern for one side so you have mirror images. Leave excess fabric around the top pieces for stitching. Use the same method to mark the bottom fabric and interfacing pieces, and cut out.

2 Assemble the large piece of top fabric in the hoop (see *Techniques*, page 109). Fill in each heart with a continuous line of split stitch, beginning on the outside of the heart and working your way toward the center. I used a variety of colors for the hearts.

3 Use back stitch to outline each heart in black pearl cotton.

4 Use a hot iron to press out any wrinkles left by the embroidery hoop. Cut out the embroidered pieces along the marked lines.

5 Join the top pieces together with right sides facing and machine stitch along the straight side with a ½-in. (12-mm) seam allowance.

6 Press the seams open. Join the two bottom pieces of the collar in the same way.

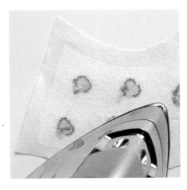

7 Lay the pieces of interfacing on the back of the embroidered pieces of collar, with the rough side facing down, and press lightly with the iron to fuse.

8 Put the top and bottom pieces of the collar together, with the right sides facing in. Position one tie in each corner, as shown, with the longer ends running in between the fabric layers. Pin around the edges and where the tie is positioned to hold everything in place.

9 Machine stitch around the edge of the collar with a 1/2-in. (12-mm) seam allowance, using the edge of the interfacing as a guide. Leave a 3-in. (7.5-cm) opening in the center of the smaller curve for turning the collar right side out.

10 Trim the seam allowance to 1/4 in. (6 mm), clip the corners, making sure not to cut into any of your stitches, and carefully snip a few short notches into the curved edges.

11 Turn the collar right side out through the opening, using a point turner or other pointed object to push out the seams and corners. Tuck the edges of the opening inside. Press the edges with a hot iron.

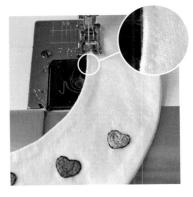

12 Hand- or machine-stitch the opening of the collar closed, then trim the ties to the desired length and knot the ends.

WATERMELON SUNGLASSES CASE

Protect your sunglasses from scratches with this playful case. The watermelon motif will serve as a reminder of summer days, while the flexible frame will keep the glasses securely tucked inside. This case is also great for holding embroidery supplies for small projects or for keeping other things together in a purse. Feel free to play with the stitches shown—long and short, chain, or back stitch are all great options for the fill, or stick with simple outlines instead.

MATERIALS

- Transfer and marking tools
- Outer fabric: ¼-yd (¼-m) piece of duck cloth or canvas
- Lining fabric: ⅓-yd (⅓-m) piece of patterned cotton fabric
- Light- to medium-weight fusible interfacing
- 7-in. (18-cm) embroidery hoop
- Cotton embroidery floss
- Embroidery needle
- Scissors
- Ruler
- Iron
- Sewing pins
- Sewing machine
- Sewing thread (to match the fabric)
- Point turner or other pointed object, e.g., chopstick, knitting needle
- 4-in. (10-cm) metal flex frame
- Pliers

STITCH USED

- Split stitch (see page 111)

THREAD COLORS USED

- Black, 4 strands
- Ecru, 6 strands
- Golden olive, 6 strands
- Melon, 6 strands

FINISHED SIZE

- 7¾ x 4 in. (19.5 x 10 cm)

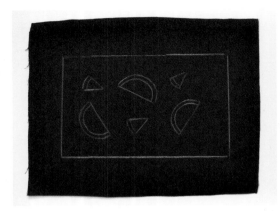

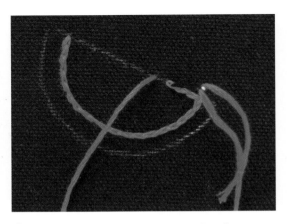

1 Enlarge the main piece (see *Templates*, page 123) by 200 percent. Transfer the watermelon motif onto one outer fabric piece only. Use the same template to mark and cut two pieces of liner fabric and two pieces of interfacing. Enlarge the tab piece by 200 percent, transfer onto the outer fabric, and cut out.

2 Assemble the piece of outer fabric with the marked design in the hoop (see *Techniques*, page 109) and stitch the central section of the watermelon motifs, using split stitch to fill the shapes completely.

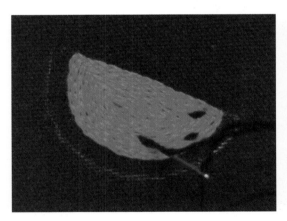

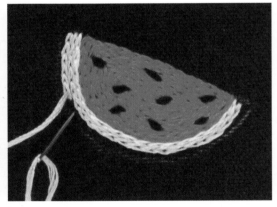

3 Add seeds to the slices of watermelon by placing single split stitches in black randomly throughout each motif.

4 Add the white and green parts of the slices by placing a single line or two of split stitch per color along the edge of the red stitching. Cut the embroidered piece of fabric and the blank piece of outer fabric to size along the marked lines of the rectangle, and set aside.

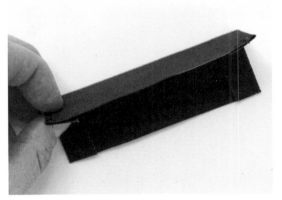

5 Take one of the tab pieces and fold in both short sides by ½ in. (12 mm). Machine-stitch the folds in place on both sides, ⅛ in. (3 mm) from the edge. The resulting piece should measure approximately 4 x 2¾ in. (10 x 7 cm).

6 Fold the tab in half, with the right side facing out, so it now measures approximately 4 x 1⅜ in. (10 x 3.5 cm). Repeat the folding and stitching process for the other tab. Set both tabs aside.

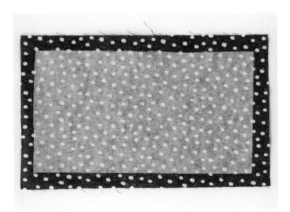

7 Use the iron to fuse the pieces of interfacing to the wrong side of the pieces of lining fabric.

8 Place the stitched piece of fabric down with the embroidered side facing up. Place one lining piece over the stitched piece, with the right side facing in.

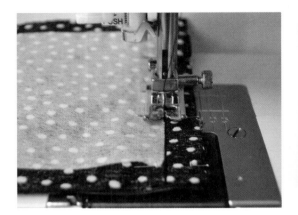

9 Sandwich one tab in between the outer and lining fabrics, centered and with the raw edges aligned. Pin the layers together. Machine stitch with a 1/2-in. (12-mm) seam allowance.

10 Remove the pins and fold the tab over toward the lining side. Topstitch 1/8 in. (3 mm) from the edge. Sew the other tab between the other pieces of outer and lining fabric in the same way.

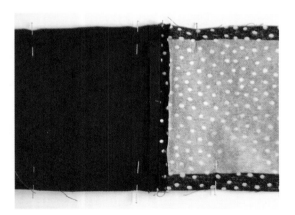

11 Place the sewn pieces together, aligning the lining sides and outer sides, as shown. Pin around the edges.

12 Machine-stitch around the entire edge, leaving a 3-in. (7.5-cm) opening in the lining for turning. Be sure not to stitch the tabs closed. Trim the edges of the fabric to 1/4 in. (6 mm).

13 Snip the corners, taking care not to snip your stitching. Turn the case right side out through the opening.

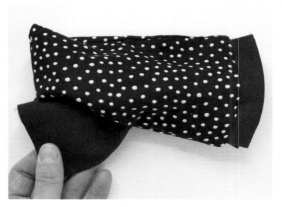

14 Use the point turner or other pointed object to push out the corners and then tuck the edges of the opening inside. Machine stitch the opening closed. Tuck the lining inside the case.

15 To insert and assemble the flex frame, open the frame on the loose side. Slide one end into each tab and push it all the way through until the ends come out on the other side.

16 Push the open hinge closed and insert the small pin that came with the flex frame kit. Use a pair of pliers to close the hinge securely.

FELT FLORAL PINS

This basic construction method can easily be used to make pins of different shapes and sizes. There's no pattern to transfer, so don't be afraid to experiment with different stitches and motifs to create your own. You'll be surprised at how quickly a few simple stitches can create a beautiful, wearable garden!

MATERIALS

- Marking tool
- Ruler
- Piece of wool or wool-blend felt
- Cotton embroidery floss
- Embroidery needle (larger sizes work best on felt)
- Fabric scissors
- Sewing pins
- Bar pin
- Hot glue gun

FINISHED SIZE

- Diameter: Approx. 1¼ in. (3 cm)

STITCHES USED

- Back stitch (see page 114)
- French knot (see page 112)
- Split stitch (see page 111)
- Straight stitch (see page 111)

THREAD COLORS USED (FOR PIN SHOWN)

- Carnation, 4 strands
- Ecru, 6 strands
- Golden olive, 4 strands
- Navy blue, 4 strands
- Topaz, 6 strands

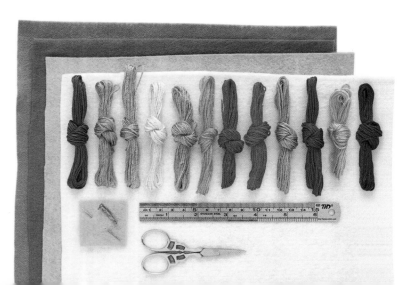

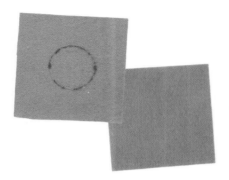

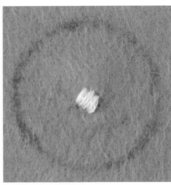

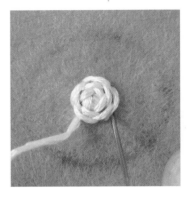

1 Cut out two 3 x 3-in. (7.5 x 7.5-cm) squares of felt. Lightly mark a 1-in. (2.5-cm) circle in the center of one of the pieces of felt.

2 To make the central rose, sew three straight stitches in the center of the circle.

3 Surround the straight stitches with other slightly overlapping straight stitches, as shown. Continue overlapping the stitches, increasing your stitch length as the rose grows, until it reaches a diameter of approximately ⅜ in. (10 mm).

4 The leaves on the left are made up of clusters of straight stitches. Start at the longest point and make a series of straight stitches to form a leaf shape. Bring the needle down at the same point for each stitch.

5 To make the berries, sew a few French knots along the bottom of the rose.

6 To make the leaves on the right, sew pairs of short straight stitches to form tiny V shapes, stacked closely together.

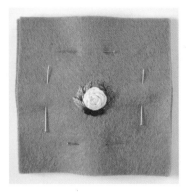

7 Pin the two layers of felt together.

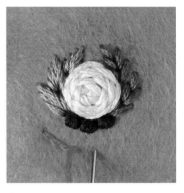

8 Split stitch around the marked circle to join the layers of felt. Finish with a few back stitches through the back layer, pass your thread between the two layers of felt, and trim.

9 Use a pair of sharp fabric scissors to trim closely around the split-stitched border.

10 Use the hot glue gun to fix the bar pin to the back of the felt pin. (You can also stitch the pin in place, but this is best done before joining the layers of felt together.)

TIP *There's no pattern to transfer, so feel free to get creative using the stitches and motifs in this book for inspiration and with different shapes and sizes of felt!*

PATTERN-PLAY PENDANT

In this pendant, I've combined a simple pattern with a bright pop of color for a fun mix of classic and contemporary. I love how the vivid color and bold pattern play on a neutral background, but feel free to experiment with different colors and textures to suit your wardrobe. These miniature wooden frames are my favorite things to work with—each tiny hoop inspires endless possibilities!

MATERIALS

- 5 x 5-in. (13 x 13-cm) square of cotton fabric in a natural color
- 3-in. (7.5-cm) embroidery hoop
- 1½-in. (4-cm) round wooden frame necklace kit
- Pencil
- Ruler
- Cotton embroidery floss
- Embroidery needle
- Fabric scissors
- Hot glue gun
- Flat-head screwdriver
- Wood glue
- Clothespins or a heavy book

STITCHES USED

- Straight stitch, for Versions A and B (see page 111)
- French knot, for Version C (see page 112)
- Satin stitch (see page 113)

THREAD COLORS USED

- Black, 4 strands
- Red (Version A), Desert sand (Version B), or Aquamarine (Version C), 4 strands

FINISHED SIZE

- Hoop diameter: Approx. 1½ in. (4 cm)
- Chain length: Approx. 27½ in. (70 cm)

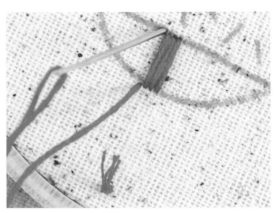

1 Assemble the fabric in the hoop (see *Techniques*, page 109). Draw a circle onto your fabric, using the round wooden center plate from your necklace kit as a guide. Using a ruler, mark a straight line across the lower quarter of the circle. Mark a pattern onto the larger section—dashes, dots, and stripes are all fun options! You can also stitch your pattern freehand if you'd like.

2 Make an away waste knot (without weaving the thread tails—see *Techniques*, page 110) 1 in. (2.5 cm) outside of the circle. Bring your needle up in the center of the bottom section's edge and work satin stitch toward one side. Once filled, return to the center and complete the other side.

TIP *Be sure to begin and end each new piece of thread with an away waste knot. This will help keep your work smooth and bump-free.*

3 Fill in the pattern as desired. Here, I've used straight stitch worked at random angles, i.e., seed stitch.

For Version C, fill in the top portion of the motif with French knots.

4 Remove the fabric from the hoop. Center the stitched design over the wooden disc from the necklace kit. Place the necklace frame directly over the stitched design and wooden disc, and push down to secure.

5 Use sharp fabric scissors to trim away the excess thread and fabric, leaving approximately ¼ in. (6 mm) of fabric around the outside of the frame.

6 Use the hot glue gun to secure the fabric and loose threads to the wooden disc at the back of the frame.

7 Assemble the hardware from the necklace kit, making sure the design is nicely aligned before fully tightening the screws with a screwdriver.

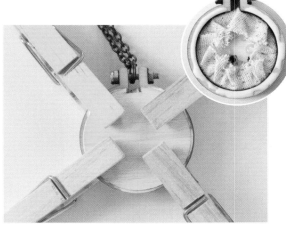

8 Apply a thin line of wood glue around the edge of the frame at the back. Align the thin wooden backing piece with the notch at the top of the frame and press firmly into place. To ensure a secure bond, clamp the pieces together with clothespins while the necklace dries. Alternatively, you can place the frame under a heavy book.

TOTE BAG WITH POM-POM CHARM

I have a collection of canvas tote bags and always find myself reaching for one in place of a handbag. They're casual and washable, and they offer plenty of room for various odds and ends. Plain totes are super affordable and offer a perfect blank canvas for some easy embellishment, turning a boring bag into a personal statement piece. Here, a stitched message of "kindness" paired with a fun and fluffy pom-pom charm is sure to spread joy as you run around town.

MATERIALS

- Transfer and marking tools
- Natural canvas tote bag
- 7-in. (18-cm) embroidery hoop
- Cotton embroidery floss
- Embroidery needle
- Iron
- 3-in. (7.5-cm) piece of ½-in. (12-mm) wide natural cotton ribbon (optional)
- Sewing pins
- Sewing machine
- Sewing thread (to match the bag)
- Yarn in assorted colors (for making the pom-poms)
- Pom-pom maker or 4 x 3-in. (10 x 7.5-cm) piece of sturdy cardstock
- Scissors
- Large clasp with jump ring
- Yarn needle
- 20-mm unfinished wood bead

STITCH USED

- Split stitch (see page 111)

THREAD COLOR USED

- Black, 6 strands

1 Transfer the "kindness" motif (see *Templates*, page 122) to the bag, centering the design near the top (see *Techniques*, pages 107–108). Assemble the top layer of the bag in the hoop (see *Techniques*, page 109). Sew with split stitch. Remove from the hoop and press out any wrinkles with an iron.

2 You can attach the charm directly to the handle of the bag. Or, to make a little tab, fold the piece of cotton ribbon in half and tuck in the ends by about ½ in. (12 mm). Pin the tab to the bag, close to where the strap attaches to the bag. Machine stitch the tab in place a few inches from the top.

3 To make the pom-poms, wrap the yarn several times around the pom-pom maker or piece of cardstock.

4 Cut an 18-in. (45-cm) piece of yarn and fold it in half to form a long loop. Carefully slide the wrapped yarn off the pom-pom maker, holding it firmly to make sure no pieces come loose.

5 Carefully wrap the loop around the middle of the bundle of yarn and tuck the loose ends through the loop. Pull tight.

6 Separate the loose ends and, holding one end in place, wrap the other several times around the middle of the yarn bundle. Tie the ends together. Be sure to tie the ends as tightly as possible—a loose tie will result in your pom-pom falling apart!

7 Cut the loops using a pair of sharp scissors. Trim your pom-pom to the desired size and shape. Repeat Steps 3-6 to make as many pom-poms as you'd like for your bag.

TIP *To make a pom-pom with different blocks of color, wrap different colors of yarn in separate sections. To make a speckled pom-pom, wrap different colors of yarn simultaneously.*

8 Cut a piece of yarn long enough to string twice through all the pom-poms, plus a few extra inches. Fold it in half to form a loop. Place the loop through the center of the jump ring and tuck through the loose ends. Pull. Thread both ends of yarn through the yarn needle.

9 Thread the pom-poms, one at a time, onto the yarn.

TIP *Make sure to push your needle directly through the center of the pom-pom. If you have difficulty pulling the needle through the pom-pom with both ends threaded at once, you can pull each strand individually.*

10 Once you've threaded all of the pom-poms, thread the wood bead onto the yarn needle and then onto the yarn. Adjust the spacing of the pom-poms and the total length of the charm, then tie a knot at the end of the yarn to secure everything in place.

11 Trim the ends of the yarn as required. Clip your charm to the tab you attached in Step 2, or directly to the bag handle.

ZIPPERED MAKEUP CASE

Zippered cases are a must for just about everything—not just for makeup. They make great gifts, especially when personalized, and are perfect for stashing portable embroidery supplies for on-the-go projects. Combining a simple outline stitch with brightly painted details lends a fun pop-art feel to this multipurpose case.

MATERIALS

- Transfer and marking tools
- Exterior fabric: two pieces of duck cloth or canvas, one measuring 7$\frac{1}{2}$ x 10$\frac{3}{4}$ in. (20 x 28 cm) and one measuring 12 x 12 in. (30$\frac{1}{2}$ x 30$\frac{1}{2}$ cm)
- Interior fabric: two pieces of patterned cotton measuring 7$\frac{1}{2}$ x 10$\frac{3}{4}$ in. (20 x 28 cm)
- Ruler
- Acrylic paint (I used Apple Barrel brand in Fuchsia and Pumpkin Orange and Americana brand in Cinnamon Drop, Poodleskirt Pink, and Vivid Violet)
- Paintbrush with short bristles
- 10-in. (25-mm) embroidery hoop
- Cotton embroidery floss
- Embroidery needle
- Iron
- Fabric scissors
- 9-in. (23-cm) zipper
- Sewing pins or binder clips
- Sewing machine (with zipper foot)
- Sewing thread (to match the exterior fabric)
- Masking tape (optional)

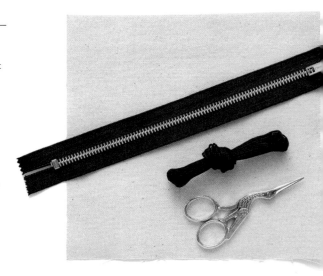

STITCH USED

- Back stitch (see page 114)

THREAD COLOR USED

- Black, 3 strands

FINISHED SIZE

- Approx. 10$\frac{3}{4}$ x 7$\frac{1}{2}$ in. (27 x 19 cm)

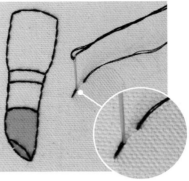

1 Enlarge the template (see *Templates*, page 119) by 250 percent and transfer the motif and outer rectangle to one exterior piece of fabric (see *Techniques*, pages 107-108). Leave excess fabric around the rectangle to allow for hoop assembly. Use the same template to mark and cut the remaining exterior and liner pieces.

2 Carefully paint the colorful part of each lipstick motif, using one or two thin coats of paint per lipstick. Allow the paint to dry completely.

3 Assemble the painted fabric in the embroidery hoop (see *Techniques*, page 109). Use back stitch to sew the black outlines of the lipstick design.

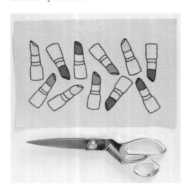

4 Remove the fabric from the hoop. Iron the fabric, with the painted side facing down, to remove any wrinkles left by the hoop. Trim to size, following the lines marked in Step 1.

5 Place the fabric right side up and align the zipper face down along the top edge. Place one piece of interior fabric, with the right side facing down, on top of the zipper, as shown.

6 Pin or clip the pieces together and sew in place, using a sewing machine with a zipper foot, and making sure to move the zipper pull out of the way as you sew.

TIP *Duck cloth frays very easily, so it is a good idea to line the edges of the larger exterior piece of fabric with masking tape. The tape will keep the edges intact while you paint and embroider.*

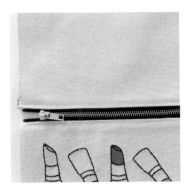

7 Flip the fabric over, so that the right sides are facing outward, and press with a hot iron, pushing the fabric away from the zipper on each side. Topstitch the pressed layers together along the zipper.

8 Repeat Steps 6-7 to make the other side of the case, using the remaining pieces of exterior and interior fabric.

9 Open the zipper three-quarters of the way. (Don't forget this part or you won't be able to turn your case right side out!) Flip the fabric over, so that the right sides of the exterior and the right sides of the interior fabric are together. Make sure the zipper teeth are pointing toward the interior fabric.

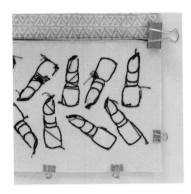

10 Pin or clip the edges together. Sew along all four sides with a ½-in. (12-mm) seam allowance, leaving an opening of 4-5 in. (10-12 cm) at the bottom of the interior layer for turning.

11 Clip the corners with sharp scissors, making sure not to clip into your stitches, then turn the pouch the right side out through the opening in the interior layer.

12 Fold the raw edges of the opening inward and sew closed. Tuck the liner into the outer pouch and push out the corners.

HAND AND NEEDLE PATCH

Patches are a great way to express your personality; they can transform an ordinary garment into a personalized fashion statement. They're a great alternative to stitching directly onto a garment, since they don't alter it permanently. The hand holding a needle and thread will declare your love for the DIY, but don't stop there—this technique can be used to make patches of any shape and size! When choosing a garment to embellish with patches, be sure to select one that won't need to be laundered heavily, such as a jacket or backpack. Once your garment has patches attached, take extra care and spot-clean or handwash and line dry only.

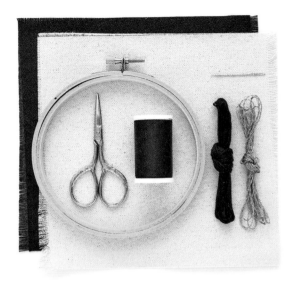

MATERIALS

- Transfer and marking tools
- 8 x 8-in. (20 x 20-cm) square of duck cloth or canvas
- 6 x 6-in. (15 x 15-cm) square of wool or wool-blend felt
- 5-in. (13-cm) embroidery hoop
- Cotton embroidery floss
- Embroidery needle
- Scissors
- Permanent fabric adhesive (washable)
- Small paintbrush or foam brush
- Sewing thread (to match the felt)

STITCHES USED

- Back stitch (see page 114)
- Running stitch (see page 114)

THREAD COLORS USED

- Black, 3 strands
- Light gold, 3 strands

FINISHED SIZE

- Approx. 4 x 4 in. (10 x 10 cm)

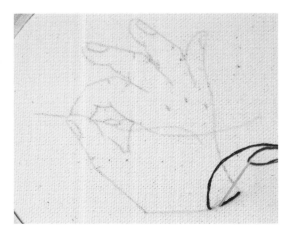

1 Transfer the hand motif (see *Templates*, page 122) to the piece of duck cloth or canvas (see *Techniques*, pages 107-108). Assemble the fabric in the hoop (see *Techniques*, page 109). Stitch the motif as shown, using back stitch with three strands of black floss for the hand and needle.

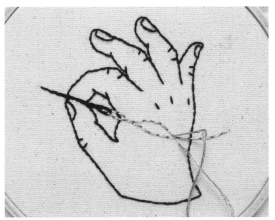

2 Use three strands of gold floss for the piece of decorative sewing thread.

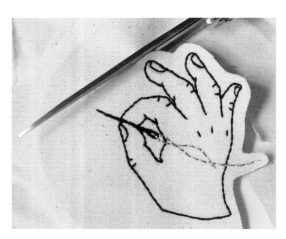

3 Remove the stitched fabric from the hoop and carefully cut out the hand motif approximately ¼ in. (6 mm) from the line of black stitches.

4 Use the paintbrush or foam brush to spread a layer of permanent fabric adhesive evenly over the back of the whole piece, making sure to get all the way to the edges. This will prevent fraying. Work as quickly as possible and add more adhesive as required as you work.

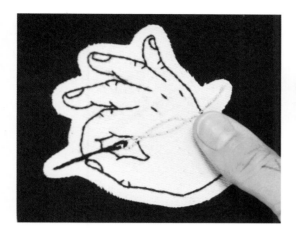

5 Place the piece of embroidered fabric, with the glue side facing down, onto the piece of felt. Press firmly in place, and wipe away any excess glue. Place the glued pieces under a book to dry for a few hours.

6 Once the adhesive has dried, carefully cut the design from the felt, leaving a 1/4-in. (6-mm) border around the edge.

7 Sew the patch onto your chosen garment using sewing thread. Use a closely spaced running stitch or back stitch, and stitch around the edge of the patch as many times as necessary until the patch is completely secure.

TIP *If the back of your embroidery is especially bulky, or if you prefer more security, you can stitch the embroidered fabric directly to the felt instead. Just choose a coordinating thread color and use your preferred stitch around the edge. If you use this method, I'd recommend applying a fray preventer sealant to the edges of the embroidered fabric before you stitch to prevent fraying.*

TECHNIQUES AND STITCH DIRECTORY

This section covers working
with templates, transfer
techniques, stabilizers,
and assembling hoops. This
chapter also illustrates
how to form all of the stitches
used to create the projects in
this book. Each stitch is
clearly explained with step-by-
step instructions and helpful
diagrams, with finished
examples of the stitch to
show how it can be applied.

WORKING WITH TEMPLATES AND MOTIFS

To use a motif exactly as it
appears at the back of the
book, just trace it onto a
sheet of tracing paper and
transfer the design to your
piece of fabric.

TRACING PAPER
Place a sheet of tracing
paper over the motif and
trace the design with a
pencil. Remove the tracing
paper and, if necessary,
darken the traced lines by
going over them with a fine-
tip marker or pen. Choose
whatever transfer method you
like (see pages 107-108).

TO ENLARGE OR REDUCE A MOTIF
Use a photocopier and specify
the percentage by which you
need to enlarge or reduce
the motif.

TRANSFER TECHNIQUES

1 STENCIL METHOD
This method is useful for transferring designs to ready-made garments, and it is ideal for creating repeating patterns. This method works best with bold shapes that don't have a lot of detail.

1 To create a stencil, trace the design onto a piece of cardstock, then carefully cut it out.

2 Place the cardstock stencil on top of the piece of fabric and draw around the edge, filling in any details by hand if necessary.

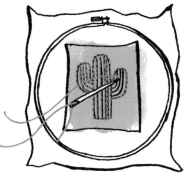

2 FREEZER PAPER METHOD
1 Use a regular pen or pencil to trace the design onto the non-shiny side of a piece of freezer paper.

2 Place the freezer paper on top of the piece of fabric, with the shiny side facing down, and then use a warm iron to temporarily stick the freezer paper to the fabric. You can then stitch directly over it.

3 Once your embroidery work is complete, gently tear away the paper in small pieces, making sure not to pull on the stitches. This method works well with materials like dark-colored felt that are tricky to mark with a pen or pencil.

3 TRACING WITH A LIGHT SOURCE

Direct tracing using a light box is probably the simplest way to transfer a design to a piece of fabric. Place the design on top of the light box, with the right side facing up, so that the design is lit from beneath. Place the piece of fabric on top of the design and position as necessary. Trace the lines of the design with the marking tool most suitable for the type of fabric you're using.

4 DRESSMAKER'S CARBON PAPER

Dressmaker's carbon paper works in the same way as ordinary carbon paper, but it is made specifically for fabric. Place the piece of fabric on a flat surface, with the right side facing up. Place the design to be traced on top of the fabric. Tuck a sheet of dressmaker's carbon paper between the fabric and the design, with the carbon side facing the fabric. Carefully trace over the design with a pencil or stylus.

5 IRON-ON PATTERN SHEETS

1 Pin the piece of fabric to a slightly padded surface. Pin the iron-on pattern sheet in place, with the ink side facing down. The design will be reversed. Use a hot iron to press down on the sheet for about 30 seconds. Do not slide the iron, but lift and replace it to cover the whole design.

2 Carefully lift one corner of the iron-on pattern sheet to see if the design has fully transferred. If not, apply more heat until all the design lines have transferred cleanly. Keep in mind that transferred lines are normally permanent and will have to be completely covered with stitches later.

NOTE Iron-on pattern sheets for these projects are provided in the envelope in the back of this book!

6 WATER-SOLUBLE STABILIZER

Designs can be traced with a pencil or printed directly onto a piece of water-soluble film or paper, which also acts as a fabric stabilizer. Pin or baste the piece of film/paper to the right side of the fabric and embroider over it. Alternatively, you can use a hoop to hold the film/paper in position against the piece of fabric. Once you've finished embroidering, rinse the fabric in water, following the manufacturer's directions, to remove all traces of the stabilizer.

STABILIZERS

Stabilizers are used underneath fabric to add weight, sturdiness, or structure. Loosely woven fabrics sometimes need to be stabilized, as might fabrics that are stretchy or very lightweight. The stabilizer is usually applied to the wrong side of the fabric prior to stitching or sewing. There are several types available, depending on what type of fabric you're working with and what the end product will be.

MUSLIN

Unbleached muslin makes a great lightweight stabilizer. When stitching a design onto cotton or linen that will be framed, adding a layer of muslin underneath adds a nice weight to the finished product and keeps messy stitches and knots from showing through to the front. Cut the muslin to the same size as the piece of fabric and assemble both layers in the hoop as one. Muslin can also be used in place of interfacing or lightweight cut- or tear-away stabilizers for projects that don't require heavy stabilizing.

INTERFACING

Interfacing is available in a variety of weights and as both fusible and sew-on types. For embroidery, lightweight-grade woven interfacing is best. Fusible interfacing is typically used for items that require machine sewing.

TEAR-AWAY OR CUT-AWAY

Tear-away stabilizers are temporary, easily removed after stitching; cut-away are permanent. Both types are available in different weights to suit different fabric weights. Cut-away stabilizer in a light- to medium-weight is a good choice for stretchy knits or loosely woven fabrics, because it provides permanent support and will prevent the design from distorting with frequent use.

ASSEMBLING AN EMBROIDERY HOOP

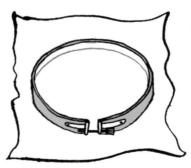

1 To assemble an embroidery hoop, adjust the screw of the outer ring so that it fits loosely over the inner ring. Place the inner ring on a flat surface, then place the fabric over the inner ring, with the area to be worked in the center.

2 Press the outer ring down over the fabric and inner ring, making sure the fabric is taut. Tighten the screw to secure the fabric.

3 Keep the fabric taut while you stitch by pulling on the edges of the fabric gently and evenly every so often, making sure not to distort the design. If you find that your fabric is slipping excessively as you stitch, try wrapping the inner ring with cotton twill tape or add a layer of muslin. Stitch or glue the ends of the tape together to keep them secure.

WORKING WITH THREADS

DIVIDING THREADS

If you plan to divide your stranded floss, begin by cutting a piece about 18 in. (45 cm) long. Hold one end of the floss in one hand and separate the strands with the other. Pull the threads out one by one and combine them to achieve the desired thickness. Make sure the threads are not twisted together, for better coverage and smoother stitching.

BEGINNING AND ENDING THREADS

1 SIMPLE KNOTS

Though traditional embroiderers would probably disapprove, I often begin and end my thread with a simple knot placed on the back of my fabric. To begin a thread in this way, simply thread your needle with a piece of thread no longer than 18 in. (45 cm) and tie a knot at one end. Bring the needle up through the piece of fabric from the back where you'd like to begin, pull the thread all the way through so that the knot is resting against the backside, and stitch away. To end a thread, push your needle back down through the fabric, then tie a knot close to the fabric. Trim the excess thread.

2 AWAY WASTE KNOTS

Away waste knots are useful if you need the back of your work to be smooth. To start a thread using an away waste knot, make a knot at the end of the thread. Bring the needle down through the fabric, a few inches from where you plan to begin stitching, and pull the thread all the way through so that the knot is resting on the right side of the fabric. When you've finished stitching, end the thread by pulling the needle and thread to the back of the fabric and weaving the tail of the thread several times through the last few stitches to secure, then snip. Pull up gently on the away waste knot and carefully snip it away, then pull the excess thread through to the back. Re-thread the thread onto your needle, then weave the tail through a few stitches to secure and snip.

PRESSING EMBROIDERED FABRIC

You might find it necessary to press your embroidered fabric to prepare it for the next stage of a project.

Lay the work face down on a padded surface. Heat the iron to a setting suitable for both the fabric and threads, with steam.

If your iron doesn't have a steam setting, dampen a lightweight cloth and place it over the embroidery when pressing to lightly steam.

Hand-block the fabric by pulling on it gently and evenly to square it up and smooth it out while it is still slightly damp from the steam. Make sure the fabric is completely dry before continuing.

TIP If you are making something that will be laundered, such as clothing or table linens, it's a very good idea to wash, dry, and iron the piece of fabric prior to embroidering in order to stop it shrinking later.

TIP It's a smart idea to keep a small container close by for storing thread scraps longer than a few inches. They're good to keep at hand for small projects where you might need to make just a few stitches.

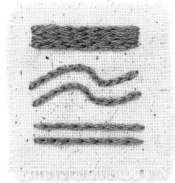

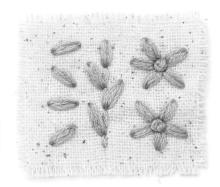

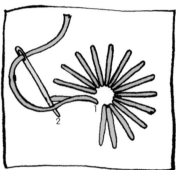

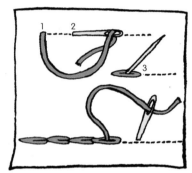

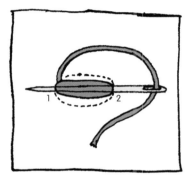

STRAIGHT STITCH

Bring the needle up at 1 and then insert it at 2. Repeat, as required.

NOTE Straight stitches of similar lengths placed close together at random angles are also referred to as seed stitch.

SPLIT STITCH

Bring the needle up at 1 and down at 2. Pull the thread through firmly. Bring the needle up again at 3, through the center of the previous stitch. Repeat, as required.

GRANITOS STITCH

Bring the needle up at 1 and down at 2. Repeat, always coming up and going down in the same holes. Continue, as required, until the stitch is the desired size.

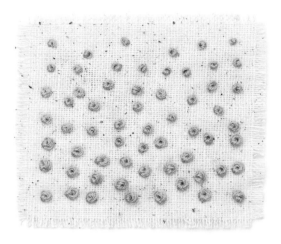

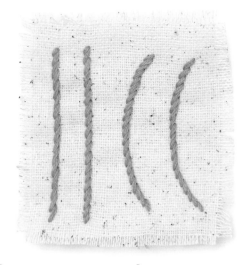

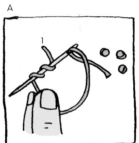
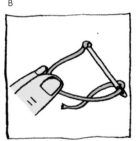
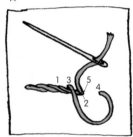
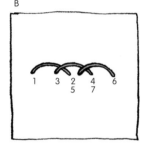

FRENCH KNOT

FIG A
Bring the needle up at 1. Holding the thread taut with the finger and thumb of your other hand, tightly wind the thread twice around the tip of the needle.

FIG B
Still holding the thread, insert the needle very close to 1 and pull it through to the back of the work, so the twists are lying neatly on the surface of the fabric. Repeat, as required.

NOTE For a smaller French knot, wrap the thread around the needle just once in Fig A. For a larger knot, wrap the thread three or four times.

STEM STITCH

FIG A
Bring the needle up at 1, down at 2, and up at 3, halfway between 1 and 2, above the stitch. Bring the needle down at 4 and up next to 2 (at 5), above the stitch. Repeat to the end of the line. Each stitch should be the same length, and begin halfway along the previous stitch.

FIG B
For a broader line, angle the needle slightly so that it is inserted below the required line and brought out just above it, a tiny distance above the end of the previous stitch.

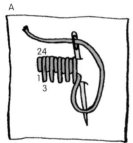

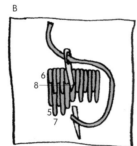

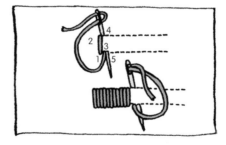

LONG AND SHORT STITCH

FIG A

Begin stitching along the outline with a row of long and short stitches: bring the needle up at 1, down at 2, up at 3, and down at 4. Repeat.

FIG B

For the second row, bring the needle up at 5, down at 6, piercing the base of the short stitch above, up at 7, and down at 8, piercing the base of the long stitch above. Repeat. Note that the stitches in the second and all subsequent rows should be the same length; only the first and last rows will actually use a combination of long and short stitches. End with a row of long and short stitches.

SATIN STITCH

Bring the needle up at 1, down at 2, up at 3, down at 4, and up at 5. Repeat, as required. The stitches should be close together, with no fabric showing between them.

NOTE For a more defined and slightly raised edge, first outline the shape with split stitch (see page 111) or stem stitch (see page 112), then satin stitch as described above, just over the stitched outline.

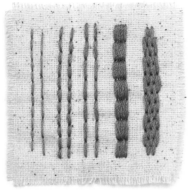

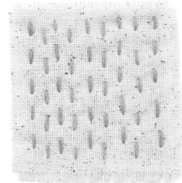

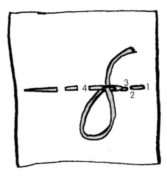

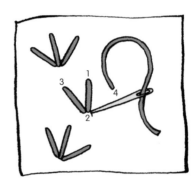

BACK STITCH

Bring the needle up at 1, down at 2, and up at 3. The distance of 1-2 should be the same as the distance of 1-3. Begin the next stitch by inserting the needle at 1 again. Repeat, as required, keeping the stitch length constant.

RUNNING STITCH

Bring the needle up at 1, down at 2, up at 3, and down at 4, ready to begin the next repeat. The stitch lengths can be kept the same for a uniform look, or varied to create a pattern.

FERN STITCH

Bring the needle up at 1 and down at 2 to make the center stitch in the required direction. Bring the needle up at 3, down at 2, up at 4, and down again at 2. Repeat, as required.

The three stitches in each group can be all the same length, with equal angles between them, or they may be varied, as required, to create foliage effects.

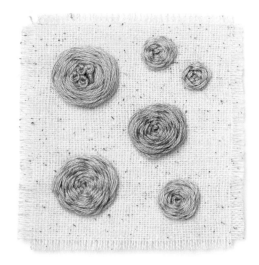

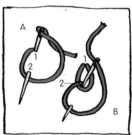

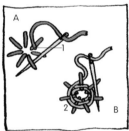

CHAIN STITCH

FIG A
Bring the needle up at 1 and insert it at
the same place, leaving a loop of thread on
the surface of the fabric. Bring the needle
up at 2, inside the loop, and down at the
same place, pulling the thread to close the
first loop while making the second. Repeat,
as required. To finish, make a tiny stitch
over the last loop to hold it in place.

DETACHED CHAIN STITCH / LAZY DAISY (FIG B):
Bring the needle up at 1 and insert it at
the same place, leaving a loop of thread on
the surface of the fabric. Bring the needle
up at 2, inside the loop, and down at a
point outside the loop, making a tiny
stitch to hold it in place. Repeat, as
required. When worked in a circle, this
is called "lazy daisy stitch."

WOVEN WHEEL STITCH

FIG A
Mark the fabric with a circle, then divide
the circle with an odd number of evenly
spaced dots. Work an odd number of radiating
stitches, or "spokes," by bringing the needle
up through each outer dot and in through the
circle. Bring a blunt needle up at 1.

FIG B
Weave over the first "spoke" and under the
next. Continue weaving, as required, until
you reach the ends of the spokes. Pull the
first few rounds of weaving tightly to
close up the center, but make later rounds
looser so that they lie flat. When the
weaving is complete, insert the needle under
the previous round of weaving (e.g., at 2)
and pull the thread through to the back of
the fabric.

hello

"HELLO" HOOP

- Pages 16–19
- $4^1/_2$ in. (11.5 cm) wide; $2^1/_8$ in. (5.4 cm) high
- Shown actual size

WILDFLOWERS HOOP

- Pages 24–27
- 4 in. (10 cm) in diameter
- Shown actual size

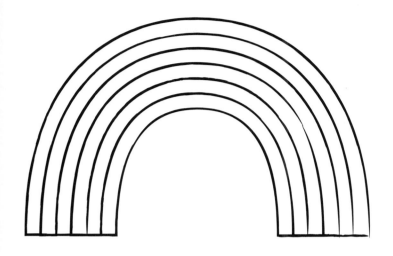

RAINBOW HOOP

- Pages 28-33
- 3½ in. (9 cm) wide; 2¼ in. (6 cm) high
- Shown actual size

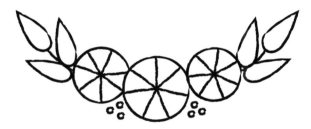

MONOGRAM HOOP

- Pages 34-37
- 3 in. (7.5 cm) wide; 1½ in. (4 cm) high
- Shown actual size

BUZZING BEES HOOP

- Pages 38-41
- 2½ in. (6.5 cm) wide; 1½ in. (4 cm) high
- Shown actual size

Positional guide

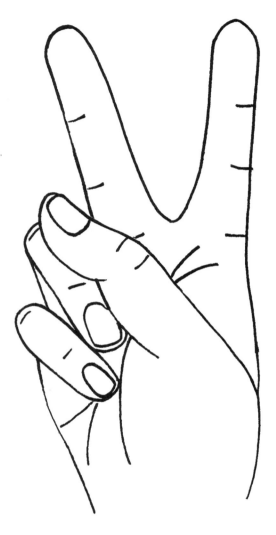

PEACE AND NAIL POLISH HOOP

- Pages 42-45
- 2½ in. (6.5 cm) wide;
  5½ in. (14 cm) high
- Shown actual size

Cactus A

CACTUS CLOTH NAPKINS

- Pages 58-61
- A: 2 in. (5 cm) wide;
  2 in. (5 cm) high
- B: 1¾ in. (4.5 cm) wide;
  2¾ in. (7 cm) high
- Shown actual size

Cactus B

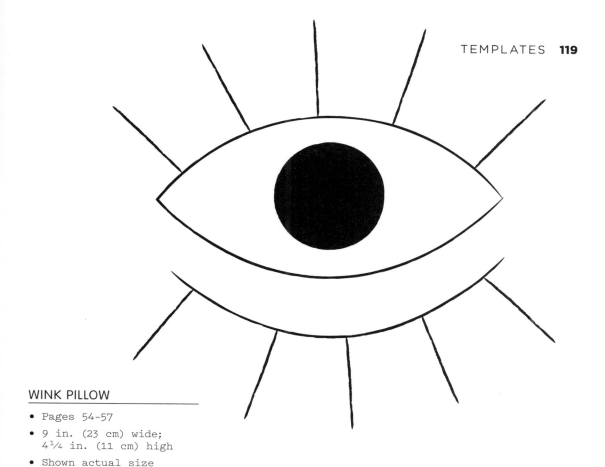

WINK PILLOW

- Pages 54-57
- 9 in. (23 cm) wide;
  4¼ in. (11 cm) high
- Shown actual size

ZIPPERED MAKEUP CASE

- Pages 98-101
- ⅞ in. (22 mm) wide;
  2 in. (5 cm) high
- Shown at 40%

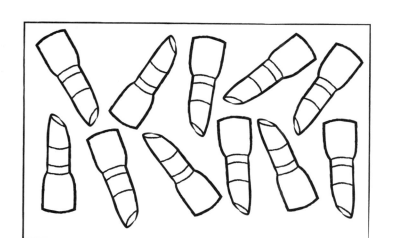

Main piece for exterior fabric (x 2) and interior fabric (x 2)

LETTER FLAG BANNER

- Pages 50-53
- Capital letter height: 1¾ in. (4.5cm)
- Shown at 39%

Aa Bb Cc Dd
Ee Ff Gg Hh Ii
Jj Kk Ll Mm Nn
Oo Pp Qq Rr
Ss Tt Uu Vv Ww
Xx Yy Zz æ ø /,
ˊ ˋ ^ ˇ ·· — ~ ˘ ˚

ALTERNATIVE ALPHABET

- For Letter Flag Banner (pages 50-53) and Tote Bag with Pom-Pom Charm (pages 94-97)
- Capital letter height: 1¾ in. (4.5 cm)
- Shown at 30%

Aa Bb Cc Dd

Ee Ff Gg Hh Ii Jj

Kk Ll Mm Nn Oo

Pp Qq Rr Ss Tt Uu

Vv Ww Xx Yy Zz

æ ø / ; ´ ` ^ ˇ .. — ~ ˘ ˚

kind- ness

TOTE BAG WITH POM-POM CHARM

- Pages 94–97
- 5½ in. (14 cm) wide; 5 in. (13 cm) high
- Shown actual size

HAND AND NEEDLE PATCH

- Pages 102–105
- 2¾ in. (7 cm) wide; 3¼ in. (8 cm) high
- Shown actual size

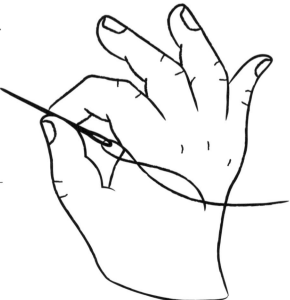

WATERMELON SUNGLASSES CASE

- Pages 80-85

Main piece for outer fabric (x 2), liner fabric (x 2), and interfacing (x 2): 5 in. (13 cm) high; 8 in. (20 cm) wide

Cut (for outer and liner fabric)

Interfacing (for interfacing pieces)

Shown at 50%

Tab piece for outer fabric (x 2): 2¾ in. (7 cm) high; 5 in. (13 cm) wide

cut

Shown at 50%

STRIPED PLANT COZY

- Pages 62-65
- Shown at 23%

Main piece for outer fabric (x 2) and liner fabric (x 2)

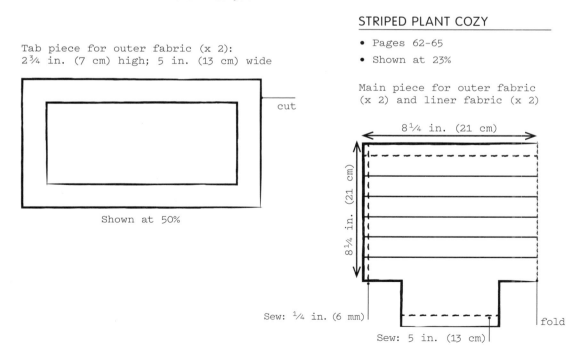

8¼ in. (21 cm)

8¼ in. (21 cm)

Sew: ¼ in. (6 mm)

Sew: 5 in. (13 cm)

fold

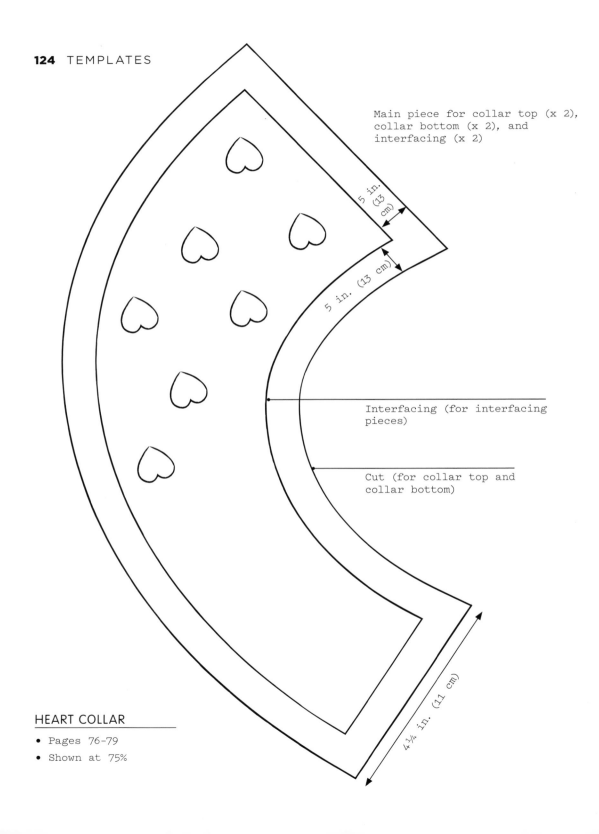

Main piece for collar top (x 2),
collar bottom (x 2), and
interfacing (x 2)

5 in. (13 cm)

5 in. (13 cm)

Interfacing (for interfacing
pieces)

Cut (for collar top and
collar bottom)

4¼ in. (11 cm)

HEART COLLAR

- Pages 76-79
- Shown at 75%

LETTER FLAG BANNER

- Pages 50-53
- 4 in. (10 cm) high; 3 in. (7.5 cm) wide
- Shown at 50%

FRAMED FERN

- Pages 66-69
- 4¼ in. (11 cm) high; 6¼ in. (16 cm) wide
- Shown at 75%

FLORAL JACKET

- Pages 72-75
- Small flowers: 1½ in. (4 cm) in diameter
- Medium flowers: 2½ in. (6.5 cm) in diameter
- Large flowers: 3½ in. (9 cm) in diameter
- Large leaves: 2 in. (5 cm) long
- Small leaves: 1½ in. (4 cm) long
- Shown at 75%

INDEX

DMC THREADS

Many thanks to DMC, who generously supplied the embroidery thread used in this book. Founded in France in 1746, DMC still makes the world's favorite embroidery cotton at its iconic factory in Mulhouse. Wherever people stitch, you'll find award-winning DMC threads uniting generations of discerning needleworkers and passionate crafters. Discover more at dmc.com

"Hello" Hoop
- DMC 832 Golden Olive
- DMC 917 MD Plum

Confetti Hoop
- DMC 3341 Apricot
- DMC 943 MD Aquamarine
- DMC 892 MD Carnation
- DMC Ecru
- DMC 564 V LT Jade
- DMC 444 DK Lemon
- DMC 917 Plum
- DMC Light Effects Precious Metals E3821 Light Gold
- DMC 796 DK Royal Blue
- DMC 761 LT Salmon
- DMC 519 Sky Blue
- DMC 554 LT Violet

Wildflowers Hoop
- DMC 351 Coral
- DMC Ecru
- DMC 832 Golden Olive
- DMC 895 V DK Hunter Green
- DMC 754 LT Peach
- DMC 580 DK Moss Green
- DMC 3820 DK Straw
- DMC 780 Ultra V DK Topaz

Rainbow Hoop
- DMC 3341 Apricot
- DMC 504 V LT Blue-Green
- DMC 892 MD Carnation
- DMC 950 LT Desert Sand
- DMC 917 MD Plum
- DMC 152 MD LT Shell Pink

Monogram Hoop
- DMC 504 V LT Blue-Green
- DMC Ecru
- DMC 832 Golden Olive
- DMC 3801 V DK Melon
- DMC 754 LT Peach
- DMC 3820 DK Straw

Buzzing Bees Hoop
- DMC 310 Black
- DMC 3820 DK Straw
- Pearl cotton, black, size 12

Peace and Nail Polish Hoop
- DMC 310 Black
- DMC 666 Bright Red

Letter Flag Banner
- DMC 943 MD Aquamarine
- DMC 666 Bright Red
- DMC 351 Coral
- DMC 754 LT Peach
- DMC Light Effects Precious Metals E3821 Light Gold
- DMC 3820 DK Straw

Wink Pillow
- DMC 310 Black

Cactus Cloth Napkins
- DMC 310 Black

Striped Plant Cozy
- DMC 310 Black
- DMC Ecru

Framed Fern
- DMC 943 MD Aquamarine

Floral Jacket
- DMC 3727 LT Antique Mauve
- DMC 3341 Apricot
- DMC 504 V LT Blue-Green
- DMC 666 Bright Red
- DMC 351 Coral
- DMC 832 Golden Olive
- DMC 732 Olive Green
- DMC 917 MD Plum
- DMC 152 MD LT Shell Pink
- DMC 3820 DK Straw

Heart Collar
- DMC 3727 LT Antique Mauve
- DMC 666 Bright Red
- DMC 791 V DK Cornflower Blue
- DMC 958 DK Seagreen
- DMC 964 LT Seagreen
- DMC 754 LT Peach
- DMC 3820 DK Straw
- Pearl cotton, black, size 12

Watermelon Sunglasses Case
- DMC 310 Black
- DMC Ecru
- DMC 834 V LT Golden Olive
- DMC 3801 V DK Melon

Felt Floral Pins
- DMC 892 MD Carnation
- DMC Ecru
- DMC 832 Golden Olive
- DMC 823 DK Navy Blue
- DMC 780 Ultra V DK Topaz

Pattern-Play Pendant
- DMC 310 Black
- DMC 943 MD Aquamarine
- DMC 666 Bright Red
- DMC 950 LT Desert Sand

Tote Bag with Pom-Pom Charm
- DMC 310 Black

Zippered Makeup Case
- DMC 310 Black

Hand and Needle Patch
- DMC 310 Black
- DMC Light Effects Precious Metals E3821 Light Gold

CREDITS

For Clair, Henry, and Jack. Thank you for putting up with all of the lost needles in the couch. You are my everything.

A special thanks to photographer, Tori Watson, who took the images of me on pages 7, 8, and 9.